FIFE COUNCIL LIBRARIES

D1339159

Howar   ker,
anthropologist a   Ph.D. he
lived for two yea   Amazon
basin, and as a f   eral months
with the Tuareg *ou for using your li*a as well as
unde taking many Library *prments* around the world.
His revious books a. *. Search of the Immortals*, about
m *a* ny cultures around the world, and *Arthur the
Dr a n King*, which traced the roots of the King Arthur
lege d back to the nomadic warrior peoples of central
Asia

www.**booksattransworld**.co.uk

DAD'S WAR

HOWARD REID

BANTAM BOOKS

LONDON • NEW YORK • TORONTO • SYDNEY • AUCKLAND

DAD'S WAR
A BANTAM BOOK: 0 553 81554 7

Originally published in Great Britain by Bantam Press,
a division of Transworld Publishers

PRINTING HISTORY
Bantam Press edition published 2003
Bantam edition published 2004

3 5 7 9 10 8 6 4 2

Copyright © Howard Reid 2003

The right of Howard Reid to be identified as the author of
this work has been asserted in accordance with sections 77
and 78 of the Copyright Designs and Patents Act 1988.

Condition of Sale
This book is sold subject to the condition that it shall not,
by way of trade or otherwise, be lent, re-sold, hired out or
otherwise circulated in any form of binding or cover other
than that in which it is published and without a similar
condition including this condition being imposed on the
subsequent purchaser.

Set in Granjon by
Falcon Oast Graphic Art Ltd.

Bantam Books are published by Transworld Publishers,
61–63 Uxbridge Road, London W5 5SA,
a division of The Random House Group Ltd,
in Australia by Random House Australia (Pty) Ltd,
20 Alfred Street, Milsons Point, Sydney, NSW 2061, Australia,
in New Zealand by Random House New Zealand Ltd,
18 Poland Road, Glenfield, Auckland 10, New Zealand
and in South Africa by Random House (Pty) Ltd,
Endulini, 5a Jubilee Road, Parktown 2193, South Africa.

Papers used by Transworld Publishers are natural, recyclable
products made from wood grown in sustainable forests. The
manufacturing processes conform to the environmental
regulations of the country of origin.

Printed and bound in Great Britain by
CPI Antony Rowe, Chippenham and Eastbourne

For Mum

FIFE COUNCIL LIBRARIES	
HJ201136	
HJ	26-May-2010
920H~W REI	£10.99
WARS	AANF

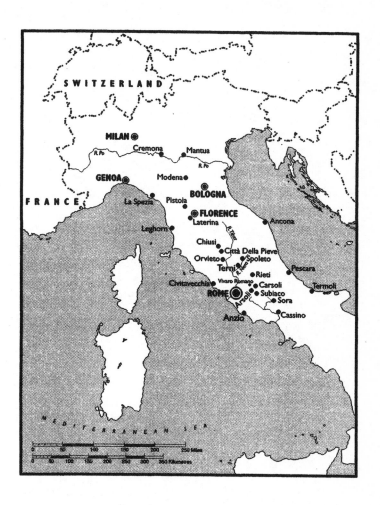

CHAPTER ONE

SPRING 1957

THE CLOCK SAYS IT'S SEVEN THIRTY IN THE MORNING. I'VE been gazing at the flowery patterns on my curtains for the past hour, but now I'm allowed to get up. I spring well clear of the tigers and wolves under the bed, saddle up my trusty charger Champion and gallop into my parents' bedroom. It's nearly filled by their giant bed, which I take by assault down the centre. The blankets are coarse and cream-coloured, topped with a light-green nylon eiderdown, though the sheets are crisp white linen.

'Good morning, Dad*dee*!' I bellow, drawing myself up and offering a full parade salute.

There is no reply.

Dad is just sitting there, staring out into space. I touch his forehead. It's cold and wet with sweat. His skin is all grey, with yellow blotches.

'What's the matter, Daddy?' I snuggle down in the centre of the bed, next to him, nuzzling him. Why is he like this? An arm and hand descend lightly round my shoulders – his left hand, the good one, with no bullet holes. It makes me feel better, but I'm still scared. Why is Death suddenly trying to get Daddy?

'Don't worry, Howard dear. Daddy's just had one of his nightmares about the war. He'll be fine in a minute,' Mum says.

But I don't understand at all. Only yesterday, out walking, Dad was telling us all about the great fun he had in the war: eating all those grapes and yummy ham and spaghetti . . . the pretty Italian girls with scarves over their hair who looked after him . . . the horrid Germans he always managed to get away from. Simon and Jan and I love it all so much we are almost there with him. We practise marching, and singing 'Lili Marlene' and 'Santa Lucia' with him on the way home.

But now he's shaking and wet and the smell from under his arms is bitter and he can't talk. I decide to stay with him, to guard him in his bed until Mum calls that his bath is drawn. I dive across the room and haul his dressing gown down from the back of the door. I am rewarded with a thin smile. I cling to his leg. At least Death hasn't got him this time. We go to the loo together and I watch as his jet of dark yellow wee splashes steadily into the bowl. On and on seemingly endlessly, at least ten times as long as I can manage. I wonder if one day I, too, will be able to pee for such an eternity.

AUGUST 1964

DAD HAS BOUGHT A CAMPER VAN. THE PLAN IS TO DRIVE gently through France, cross the Alps like Hannibal (at about the same speed), then take the sun on Napoleon's Isle of Elba. After a week there Dad decides we should go to visit some old friends of his who live near Orvieto, friends from the war. We cross to the mainland, take the coast road south, then cut inland through the Tuscan hills to Arezzo. There we join the main motorway to Rome, the *autostrada del sole*, 'motorway of the sun'.

Except it isn't sunny. We are embroiled in one of those freak rainstorms that sometimes hit Italy in August. The rain is so heavy we have to slow down to about thirty miles an hour. We plod on, and as the rain begins to clear we find ourselves driving along a raised section of the motorway, built on giant pillars above the valley floor.

Rounding a bend, we are suddenly confronted by a huge traffic jam. There are no cars at all in the oncoming lanes, but the whole motorway is blocked solid on our side. We sit and wait. Italians climb out of their cars, craning their necks to see what's going on, chatting animatedly with one another, gesticulating passionately.

Ten minutes later a helicopter whizzes over our heads, following the motorway. It seems to stop and hover about half a mile further down the road. It's the first chopper I have seen in action, close up – blue with POLIZIA painted in white down both sides. Dad climbs out of the car and joins the crowd of drivers, gesticulating himself with his part-paralysed right hand. After a few minutes he comes back to the car and tells us there has been a bad pile-up ahead. I wonder if it involves one of the red Ferraris I'd seen hurtling past us earlier at well over a hundred miles an hour.

Two blue-uniformed *carabinieri* appear, waving,

blowing their whistles and ordering us all to turn round and drive slowly back in the direction we came from. They have sub-machine guns slung casually across their backs. Dad calls to one of them in Italian and asks what's happened. Surprised to hear a foreigner speaking Italian (albeit heavily anglicized), he takes the time to explain. Dad's face is suddenly very serious. When the policeman finishes and is organizing the other vehicles to allow us to turn, Dad tells us. The rain has been so torrential that it has caused a reservoir built into the side of the valley to burst through its retaining wall. A huge blast of water has shot down the side of the valley and ploughed into the concrete pillars holding up the motorway. Its force was so overwhelming it washed the pillars entirely away, felling the road above. Just a few minutes before we would have crossed that very stretch of road, it disappeared. Those few minutes are all that separated our entire family from extinction.

The policeman doesn't know how many cars are involved, but he thinks that at least twenty plunged into the gaping hole. We learn later that the death toll is more than thirty.

We are silent as Dad backs the camper to the edge of the motorway platform and laboriously hauls it round to join the cavalcade back to the junction we have just passed. I look down at the flimsy crash barrier separating us from the fifty-foot drop to the valley floor.

Once we are clear of the motorway Dad pulls over onto the verge and takes stock. It's as if a quite different part of his being has suddenly come to life. He folds up the road map beside him.

'No point in trying to get through to Orvieto on the

made-up roads,' he says. 'They'll all be cut on this side of the valley. Only thing to do is take the cart tracks. I know the lie of the land round here. We'll get through in a day or so. We'll stop in a village on the way and see if we can't get the locals to point us in the right direction.'

Dad is in escaper mode.

We follow the convoy of vehicles up the metalled road until he spots a narrow track running off to the right. A closer look reveals that it heads downhill back into the valley, not across the hills, so we drive on. A little further up, a wider dirt track meanders away into the distance, keeping its height across the hills. Dad nudges the camper gently off the asphalt and onto the mud. No skids or sinking feelings: the surface is hard and rocky despite the recent downpour. Bumping along at ten miles an hour, we pass intermittently through misty grey olive groves and neatly tended vineyards, though we also cross a lot of scrubland, terrain too poor to cultivate nowadays.

We take to the cart track at about four in the afternoon and an hour or so later we come to a hamlet, a huddle of brown stone houses clustered round a small church. One of the houses has chairs outside and tin signs advertising ice creams – the local bar-trattoria. Dad climbs down from the van and strolls over to a group of elderly men gathered round a table, intensely absorbed in their afternoon card game. The sight of this huge (Dad is six foot four) blue-eyed fellow in orange shorts and open sandals is enough to distract them, temporarily. After politely explaining that we are a bit lost, Dad asks them to point him to the priest's house.

The *padre* too is a little bemused by Dad's sudden arrival on his doorstep, but he quickly recovers his composure as my father explains our predicament. The priest's first gesture is to usher us into a large, empty hall, at the same time announcing that we can all sleep there that night. Then he calls in a middle-aged lady – his housekeeper, we presume – and instructs her to prepare a big bowl of pasta for us. Finally he takes Dad into his own quarters to show him a large-scale map of the area. The tracks leading to Orvieto are quite easy to follow and the *padre* gives us some good landmarks to look out for: 'When you see a big oak tree on your right, take the left fork,' and suchlike.

After a fine bowl of pasta and a good sleep in the church hall we rise early, thank the *padre* warmly for his hospitality and trundle off along the right dirt track. His directions serve us well and we make it to Orvieto well before nightfall.

The whole sequence of events gives me a queer sense of time warp, especially as I am about halfway through Dad's book, *Prisoner at Large: The Story of Five Escapes*. He wrote it after the war, before I was born, and he's only just told me that, at thirteen, I'm old enough to read it now. Then suddenly it seems to be happening to us too. A terrifyingly close encounter with death; a miraculous escape; a plan to carry us clear of trouble; delivery at the hands of a priest and a map. It's as though we are reliving one of Dad's wartime adventures. I find it thrilling but weird, as if we have been sucked up into a sort of time-loop which only spits us back out into the mid 1960s once it has run its course.

Though this is the first time we have seen Dad in full escaper mode in a real emergency and in the right setting, we all know plenty about his wartime adventures. For as long as I can remember, we've been taking long Sunday walks with him. Our destination alternates between the Red Lion and the Dog and Duck, where Dad downs a pint or two of beer and we have the Sunday treat — Cherryade or Coca Cola.

The round trip is about four miles, and all the way there and back Dad regales us with tales of his escapades in Italy during the war. He is a wonderful storyteller, with a real gift for bringing events to life. Here Special Forces sergeant Smoky hurls his escape knife into the POW camp before the German guards search him; there a group of them slip through a hole in a hedge and crawl across a cornfield after a delousing session. Dad always sings the praises of the Italian country folk who took him in, fed and clothed him, nursed him when he was sick, risked their lives for him many times. In fact, though we are most thrilled by his encounters with the dreaded Germans, and the brilliant ways he and his chums outwitted them, Dad spends almost as much time telling us about munching grapes and sweetcorn and tomatoes, and the lovely food the kind Italians gave the escapers. It all becomes a sort of mantra for us. We love those stories and badger Dad to tell and retell them until we know them off by heart.

As we drive into Orvieto I am more or less up to the same point in Dad's book. I already know most of the incidents, but I'm pleased to be putting them in the right order, getting things sorted so that the random anecdotes we learnt as kids fall into a grander scheme, the coherent tale of Dad's life on the run in Italy during the war. The book is surprisingly detailed, with dates and names of villages and families, even the individuals who looked after him. In my holiday diary I draw up a checklist and determine to tick off the places and people as we meet them.

The weather's still bad, so Dad takes us to a hotel in Orvieto. It has a TV in every room and we soon find American cartoons to watch, though they're all dubbed into Italian. Since I consider myself too old to watch cartoons, I go and fiddle with the bidet in the bathroom, earnestly trying to figure out what exactly ladies do with the jet of water that shoots vertically upwards from the centre of the bowl.

An hour or so later Mum comes and shoos all four of us children downstairs. Dad is standing in the foyer with a little man who has a shiny bald head and enormous glasses: Ilario, top of my list. We are all made to go and embrace him and kiss both his cheeks. He is stubbly and there is a lingering whiff of garlic on his breath. His eyes glisten as we are presented, almost as if he is crying. It's all very Italian, very emotional, and I don't quite see what all the fuss is about. Dad and Ilario sit and talk rapidly. I hear the word 'Botto' several times, the village where Ilario hid Dad during the war. I know it's about ten miles away: I've looked it up on the road map. *'Domani'*, I hear. Good. We'll go out there with Ilario tomorrow. Another one to tick on the list.

The talk babbles on and I notice that among the smiles and embraces there are long, drawn faces, little silences, eyes staring at shoes or the floor. I can't follow the words, but I pick up a turbulent emotional undercurrent. Dad is totally immersed in the conversation, clearly delighted to see his dear old friend, but not all the news he is getting is good, I'm sure of that.

Later we go for a walk around Orvieto's old town, which is perched on the top of a huge, sheer-sided rock. It is a magnificent sight, especially the cathedral, a gigantic structure towering over the rest of the town like an aircraft carrier in dock. Elaborately decorated on the outside, inside it's almost completely bare. There's hardly a single fresco – just gigantic walls and columns stretching skywards into infinity.

Back in the fresh air we walk down to the edge of the city, where battlements cap the cliffs. Below, the countryside rolls away, straw-coloured in the August heat. To our left is a large gate, permitting the traffic – mostly Fiat 500s – to snake down below the city walls and out into the countryside.

I slip my hand into Dad's. 'Is this where it happened?' I ask quietly.

'Yes, I think so. Just before those trees there,' he replies, squeezing my hand slightly. We both know what we are talking about and neither of us wants to say any more. It's a secret shared. A terrible event once took place on that serene hillside. We turn away and head back into town to catch up with Mum and the girls.

The next day Mum makes a picnic and we pick up Ilario early, before leaving town through the same gate Dad and I had looked down on. Having crossed a narrow valley, the camper van begins to climb laboriously into the hills beyond. A few minutes later I glance back over my shoulder and there is the city all wreathed in sunshine, its jewelled crown the cathedral standing out like a Titan among midgets. A few more bends and the metal road dissolves, leaving a dusty white track to bounce along. This culminates in a descent into a tiny hamlet, where the track peters out.

Botto looks like a fairy castle that someone has cut the back off. There's a semicircle of buildings, all interlinked, with huge walls buttressed at their base. Each of them rises four or five storeys, though the window spaces of the top two floors are open to the elements. An old wooden cart fills a lean-to shed but there's no sign of the oxen needed to pull it. No sign of tractors, dogs, chickens, yesterday's leftovers put out for the cat, no sign of life. A few weeds struggle in the gravel; the doors all look tightly locked. I can follow the gist of Ilario's explanation: everyone has left the land, gone to live in the cities; none of the families Dad knew are here any more. No electricity, no water, the school closed, *tutto abbandonato*.

I watch Dad listening politely to Ilario's catechism of desertion and abandonment, and once again I sense the turmoil under the surface. This is a place of precious memories for Dad, a place of shelter and recuperation. He's plainly upset to see it so drastically altered. Things of great importance in his life happened here, at least in the weeks and months surrounding his stay. Love and agony, hope and terror, all jumbled up together.

I can feel it intuitively, but I know too that he isn't going to let on, give us the real picture of what he went through. Soldiers, men, fathers – especially fathers – just don't talk about that sort of thing, those inner feelings. They might even, for all I know, be ashamed of them. Public confession is just not a starter.

For a moment I wish I am older, so I'd know what questions to ask him, so that the turmoil would come out of him and not stick to me. I don't want him hurting, I want him to be the towering champion and guardian of our family that he usually is. That's what fathers are for, to provide us with a gauge to measure ourselves against – pillars of strength, honesty, bravery. Here, though, I sense the echoes of pain, doubt, anguish. Is there a tacit admission of weakness, defeat, that we are all trying to cover up? Why do I feel this overpowering urge to protect him, my dad, who had always sheltered and protected me?

The spell is broken by Mum, who, in her best sergeant-major voice, orders Simon and me to carry the picnic and a large car rug down the track below the homesteads, into the woods which hid and protected Dad twenty years ago. We stop by a large, shady spring.

Lunch is just as he describes it almost daily in his book: bread, tomatoes, ham, salami – all washed down with Ilario's own red wine – followed by grapes and peaches. After the meal I dip back into the book. I especially like reading about places while I'm actually visiting them. There's a lot of talk of hidden radios, long ladders and attic hideouts, secret security and the like, but of the terror, the turmoil, I can find almost nothing. I decide to wait. There are other farmhouses to visit, friends to greet, family meals to be shared, so perhaps it will all come out in the end.

That, however, is not to be on this trip.

The next morning I come down to breakfast at the hotel and Dad is that dreadful grey colour again, sweating and shaking. Only this time Death really has come prowling, kissing. No nightmares: real death. The previous night Mum decided to phone her mother, London Gran, to let her know that we are all OK despite the floods she must have read about. London Gran is nearly beside herself; she's been trying to get hold of us for three days, ever since the police called at her house in Park Square East, London NW1. They came to tell her that Dad's mum, Granny Potter, had died in her sleep four days ago. Dad was her only child, and the cleaning lady who found her knew he was away, so she gave the police my other granny's number.

Arrangements are rapidly made, mostly by London Gran, who is a ferociously well organized psychoanalyst. Dad will take the train to Rome then fly home in time for the funeral. The rest of us will be rescued by Simon's godfather, Uncle Dob, a lovely old millionaire friend of Dad's (and patient of London Gran's). He will bring his chauffeur, Sid, who will drive us all to Milan in the camper van. From there Uncle Dob will take Mum and sisters Jan and Fiona back to London first-class, on the overnight train. Sid, Simon and I will bring the camper van back over the Alps, up the Rhone valley to Paris, then across Picardy to Calais, Dover and eventually home to the beechwoods of the Chilterns. Sid smokes, and as soon as Uncle Dob and the girls are gone he dishes out his fags. Simon and I can't believe our luck and puff contentedly, like real grown-ups, all the way across Europe.

It is the first death in our immediate family, a death we know will cut Dad deeply. His father was killed in the Great War, before Dad's second birthday, so he was brought up by Granny Potter. But we, his children, her grandchildren, are effectively cocooned from the whole event. The funeral takes place before we get home, and Mum and Dad leave us with our old nanny for a few days while they close up Granny's house. It seems that Death's snarl is not something children, even young adolescents, should be involved in. Along with all the gruesome images and memories that accompany it, the adult view seems to be that death is best swept under the carpet, ignored.

There has certainly been too much of it in Mum's and Dad's generation, in the war years. Newsreels and TV screens have flashed death into the heart of my home ever since I can remember. Scenes of appalling carnage and slaughter, the Somme and the Normandy beaches, Belsen and Auschwitz, the flayed, raw bodies of Hiroshima and Nagasaki. All these danced in front of my young eyes, yet there is little help with any of the gaping questions: Why? Who did this? What were they trying to gain? What was all this suffering for?

Answers are generally deflections: 'a long time ago . . . awful but necessary . . . all put to rest now, best not to think about it . . . not your problem . . . don't take it personally'. But I do take it personally. This war business reduces my father to a shaking wreck a decade and more after it is all supposed to have stopped. It shapes Cuba and the Cold War just as surely as it shapes my incomprehension of the whole thing. And it is personal.

Granny Potter keeps a photo of Dad on her dressing table. Taken in 1936, it shows four young officers, arms linked, decked out in the magnificent full-dress uniform of the Black Watch, claymores at their sides. Dad, the tallest, is second from the right. They smile gaily at the camera, with not a care in the world. Three of the four of them are dead, killed in the war, never having reached their thirtieth birthdays. Dad is the only survivor. After Granny dies, Dad brings the picture home and puts it on his dressing table. He tells me it reminds him of how lucky he is, to have a second half to his life. I see the joy, the vitality, in their young faces, yet I know that three of them are now nothing but dust. Has somebody just air-brushed out all the suffering and agony that brought these three young lives to their end, along with the tens of millions of their fellows who went with them? And are we, the inheritors, supposed just not to care?

The truth is that the fathers have indeed eaten bitter fruits, and their children's teeth – that is, my teeth – are indeed set on edge. Yet the air-brushing, stiff-upper-lip tendency prefer us to keep our jaws clenched, so that our shuddering teeth can neither be heard nor seen, hoping that it will all just fade away. This is not how I've been taught to address such fundamental issues. I do not want my children's teeth set on edge, or even those of their children, the third and fourth generations. I know that, sooner or later, I'll have to confront this whole business head on, go out there and try to find out what happened, what *really* happened, in sunny Italy all those years ago. That will be the only way to lay the ghost to rest.

CHAPTER TWO

11th September 1943

*The wall behind the bungalows, on this side of the
compound, was about a hundred and twenty yards long and
eight foot high. The wire was attached to iron girders,
stretched inwards along the top. At each end German sentries
kept guard, mounted on high wooden platforms and
equipped with machine guns and strong searchlights pointed
down the wall. Besides these searchlights, there was a light
every few yards along the top of the wall.*

*Over the trip wire, a couple of yards this side (beyond
which it was* verboten *to tread), and into this glare of
illumination, stepped the first and bravest candidate for
escape. He was armed with a pair of wire cutters. There was
a small ledge, near the bottom of the wall, on which he
managed to perch.*

*For what seemed an eternity, he was framed there, arms
stretched upwards, snipping at the wire on the top of the
wall. It seemed incredible that neither of the sentries in*

the boxes had seen or heard him. Any minute we expected the calm of the evening to be shattered by the splatter of machine-gun fire. At last he made a sufficient hole to pull himself up, through, and over. The Italian girls had lived up superbly to their promise. They had actually succeeded in attracting the outside sentries to their house, two hundred yards away.

There was another wire fence on the far side of the wall, so Number Two had to wait some moments while Number One cut his way through this final obstacle. A few prisoners were still walking up and down the path, scrunching their feet on the gravel to deaden the noise of the climbers. A muffled form loomed up at my side.

'That guy deserves a V.C.,' I whispered to him.

'Yes. Isn't it going magnificently?' he answered. And then, after a pause: 'I'm Number Four.'

I sympathised with him. It must have been most trying, that wait.

Number Two stepped over the trip wire and up to the wall. To us his feet seemed to make a loud scraping noise on the bricks as he went up, though probably a disinterested spectator would have heard nothing. Anyway, he got away with it.

Number Three was absolutely soundless. But, alas! a moment after he had slid over, we heard a German challenge from the other side. He had dropped practically into the arms of one of the patrolling sentries, who had evidently torn himself away from the charms of the Italian signorine.

We returned hastily indoors. Number Three was soon back with us. Fortunately for him, the German sentry had regarded his attempt as a sporting effort, not a personal affront, as our Italian guards would have done in the old

days. The Jerry had neither transfixed him with his bayonet,
nor fired his rifle. When the other Germans learnt of the
break, however, their behaviour was not nearly so
philosophical. All, on principle, opened up with their
machine guns and shots went whistling round the camp. The
German officer later informed us that next time his men
would 'shoot to kill'.

We sat around discussing the day's events, commiserating
with Numbers Two and Three, and praising the courage of
Number One. Not for hundreds of pounds would I have
stood up there in all that light and cut a hole in the wire.

'Well at any rate,' I thought, 'three people have escaped
today. And the rest of us are not in Germany – yet.'

October 2000. As the plane approaches Pisa, there is a
thunderstorm directly over the runway. A couple of vast
lightning flashes light up the interior of the cabin and
the plane jumps and lurches violently. We are catching the
southern tip of a gigantic tempest that has drowned
almost all of northern Italy, causing untold damage and
taking many lives. Once again the Tuscan sun is obscured
by Italian rain. Or is it that we bring it with us, we
phlegmatic English?

The pilot puts us down safely at the second pass. On the
ground the storm seems to have eased a little; the air is
sodden but warmer than in England. Whizzing out of the
airport in a little hire car, I drive through bursts of
torrential rain followed abruptly by clear patches. As I
head south down the coast, the sky gradually clears,
letting the blue light of the moon bathe the mountains
on my left. I aim first for the farm, which Dad bought
in 1970. It has been my second home for thirty years,

the place where I breathe my way back into Italy.

The house is half a kilometre from the road, down a bumpy dirt track that descends steeply through an avenue of pines to a small parking area ringed by cypress trees planted for Dad by Marcello. Marcello was born in the house and knows everything there is to know about the land. He looks after it for us.

As I step out into the cool, damp night, all my senses spring to life. Insects whirr, click and hum, and the resinous scent of the damp cypresses lies heavy on the air. The ground underfoot is soft, a thin carpet of pine needles overlying the compacted shale. As the wind lifts, the great pines on the drive sigh. The deep peace of the countryside, the absolute calm of rural Tuscany, wraps itself around me like a welcoming blanket. I slip down to the front door, unlock it, and throw a few light switches. All is well inside.

The house is built of local stone, rocks collected from the thirteen hectares of woods, olive groves and vineyards that surround it. Judging from the patterns of the masonry, the original farmhouse was two-up, two-down, built in the late eighteenth century. Some time later another two ups and downs were added, making a four-square, two-floor main house. All the rooms are large, airy and capped with enormous chestnut beams. On these are laid shorter chestnut rafters, which support the flat terracotta tiles which make the ceilings. The house is partly cut into the hill, making the lower floor cool in the summer. This level is the *cantina*, a set of storerooms that originally housed animals, grain, wine, oil and all manner of preserved foods.

Looking downhill from the terrace, our olive groves

give way to woods and the *Maremma*, the coastal plain below us. Beyond the plain, perhaps fifty kilometres away, the mountains re-emerge, ridge after ridge fading gradually into blues and greys as they fuse with the haze of the skyline. Dad built the terrace, and took great delight in it. He got Marcello to plant a fig tree and a black table-grapevine just below it – they're massive now – and he loved nothing better than to pick ripe fruit straight from the terrace wall. Early in the evening, he would sit out in his favourite rocking chair, cradling a 'perker' of whisky or gin. Sometimes he'd strike up a tune on his mouth-organ or sing snatches of opera in his good bass voice, or just sit, smiling slightly, soaking up the delights of his own private domain.

The land falls and rolls round the house in pronounced curves. The steeper, lower slopes are covered in scrubby woods, which are home to wild boar, porcupines, beautiful little black squirrels, badgers, tortoises, foxes and a host of bird life, including golden orioles and nightingales, who sing gloriously through the June nights. Twice I have seen an eagle soar out over the old village, riding on the thermals above the escarpment. Mum and Dad were once woken by strange noises coming from the roof at the dead of night. It sounded like someone trying to break in from above. Having hastily donned dressing gowns and slippers, they marched noisily out onto the terrace and flashed torches onto the roof, but could see nothing. Next morning they told Marcello of the strange goings-on. He giggled a little and explained that the 'intruder' was an owl hunting for lizards by poking under the roof tiles with its beak. Incidents like this peppered Mum's and Dad's life in Tuscany. Every time I arrived to visit, or met up with them on their return to England, Dad would regale me with another string of delightful vignettes of the people and creatures he had encountered that year. He had a knack for catching the magic of the place.

At night in June, when the nightingales are singing, the valley below the terrace fills with fireflies, flashing their magical lanterns on and off like some fantastical but genuine midsummer night's dream.

Though it's late and cool when I arrive in October, I nevertheless take Dad's rocking chair out onto the terrace and just sit for an hour or so on this first night back, soaking up the magic of the place.

Still unsure of exactly why I am making this journey, this private pilgrimage, I have spent the last few weeks in England piecing together the starting points. A call to the regimental archivist at the Black Watch revealed that, yes, he does know of Dad, and of his book, but there is nothing more in his records. Army files have no report by or about him. But the published sources, his own and the military histories, begin to fill in the picture.

The views through the dining-room window stretch incredibly far into the distance; it's almost as if you can reach back in time through them. So in the morning I lay my books and maps and notes out on the dining table, in the glow of the morning sun pouring in through the open window. A cool breeze stirs lazily but the valley is quiet. I must carry up a few logs for the fire this evening. A cup of English tea – one of the few British habits we do import to Tuscany – and I sink gently into a reverie.

Dad was wounded and captured on 6 April 1943. His regiment, the Black Watch, was leading the infantry assault on the Gabès Gap in Tunisia when he was taken. This battle was the last serious defensive stand mounted by Rommel's Afrika Korps before they succumbed to a pincer movement, with Montgomery's troops pressing them from the southeast while a combined British–American army hit them from the west. The sixth of April was the first day of the battle, and I vaguely remember him telling me that he was out on patrol at night, or possibly very early in the morning – the assault began at 04.30 hours. Anyway, he may have been probing the front line when he was ambushed, wounded and taken prisoner. I know little more of the circumstances of his capture – it's one of those questions I never got round to asking before it was too late. It was precipitated by a rifle bullet that entered his right hand just below his wrist, cutting right across and exiting in front of the knuckle on his first finger. Much of the hand eventually became paralysed.

Dad was not a conscript, he was a regular officer, commissioned into the Black Watch from Sandhurst in 1936. But he always gave me the impression that he was really rather a reluctant soldier. His mother, Granny Potter, remarried when he was sixteen, and his new stepfather, Major Cyril Potter, prescribed a stark choice of careers to his stepson: the army or the stock market. Dad himself wanted to be a writer or journalist but this was considered entirely unsuitable. So, rightly judging that he would have more time to pursue his writing in the army, he opted for Sandhurst. He was a bright young man and passed into the academy about seventh of the 250 or so new cadets. But his was not a military mind and he passed out somewhere near to the bottom of his year.

Around this time all the graduate cadets were trying to get accepted by the regiments of their choice. He was particularly fond of telling us how he achieved his first choice. One of Dad's best friends and a fellow graduate was Archie Wavell, son of the esteemed soldier-poet Lord Wavell. They invited Dad to join their party at the annual military point-to-point races. Dad had a reputation as a keen student of racing form, so Lord Wavell asked him to mark his card with his best tips. Dad gave Lord Wavell six winners out of eight. Two days later he received his commission into the Black Watch, or so he always claimed, with a wry giggle.

He had seen action in Palestine before the war broke out, and served on the front line in North Africa for several months before he was captured. Though he always delighted in telling us of his adventures on the run, he was reluctant to talk about his actual battlefield experiences. As kids we plied him with questions about how many Germans he killed (to our disappointment, he always maintained that he had not killed any at all), how many tanks he blew up, and suchlike, but he told us almost nothing. When I tried to press him, he was almost evasive. Mostly, he said, it was incredibly boring: lots of hanging around, masses of drilling, a few rehearsals, practices. Life in a tent was rendered more comfortable by his batman, who tended to his creature comforts. Of the actual fighting, the thing I and my brother yearned to hear most about, he said only that waiting to put in an attack was worse than the attack itself. Once you got started, he said, you stopped being scared, because you were either going to get killed or you were not. But what was it like to be actually under fire, the bullets spraying round you like in the movies, we demanded. We got no answer. Either he couldn't or he wouldn't remember.

From the military histories, however, it was not hard to piece together some of what he went through. The Black Watch was an élite infantry assault regiment, their Highland troops renowned for their ferocity in the front line. In North Africa in 1943 this meant moving forward under full enemy fire, in the heat of battle; sometimes as a spearhead, on their own out in the open; at other times, in the wake of advancing tanks. Their assaults often entailed following narrow cleared paths through minefields, with little or no cover.

Montgomery was a cautious commander who rarely attacked until he had amassed overwhelming advantage over the opposition, but that also meant that he gave the enemy time to prepare their defences. Once the attack began, the forward lines were softened up with artillery, tank fire and aerial bombardment, then it was up to the infantry to enter the maelstrom and evict the enemy from the contested ground. Inevitably the troops spearheading the assaults took heavy casualties, and junior officers like Dad were expected to lead their men into battle. By the time he was captured he was certainly a battle-hardened officer with plenty of experience of ferocious front-line action under his belt. But he was not interested in passing on the details to us. Though he admitted that waiting for an attack was the scariest part of his war, he adds in his book that waiting for some escape attempts was even more nerve-racking.

His book opens with the tersest of references to his combat role:

I was taken prisoner on April 6th 1943 in Tunisia whilst serving with the 7th Battalion of the Black Watch (51st Highland Division). The Battalion had opened the 8th Army's assault on the Gabès Gap, the position to which the Germans withdrew from the Mareth Line.

According to Montgomery's biographer, Ronald Lewin, things were a good deal rougher than Dad records, however:

... 51st Highland, though it had gained ground on the ridge, nevertheless endured such desperate counterattacks by both Germans and Italians that the Divisional Intelligence Summary stated: 'There is no doubt that the day marked the fiercest fighting that the Division has experienced in this campaign.'

Perhaps it was in one of those 'desperate counter-attacks' that he was taken, as his immediate captors were Italian. A wounded officer, he was flown to Rome, then transferred to a POW (prisoner of war) hospital in Bologna, where his hand took four months to 'heal'. I remember him telling me of the agony as an Italian doctor probed the wound, seeking out bullet fragments. Fearing that he wouldn't regain the use of the hand, he taught himself to write left-handed while he was being treated. In the end he found that he could hold a pen in his right hand, though his writing remained small and cramped thereafter. When I was little I didn't realize how important the act of writing was for him. I didn't discover until I was much older that writing had, in fact, both sustained him through some of his worst wartime experiences and played an important part in his post-war healing process.

It was a dream of his – a dream I have inherited – to spend part of his year here on the farm in Tuscany, writing. In such a wonderfully calm place, it's not difficult to draw your thoughts together, set pen to paper, begin to tease out a plot. Sometimes the wind in the pines sings out the storyline, or the whirring of the cicadas in the oaks and acacias grinds the words, like a whetstone honing a keen edge. The raucous screech of a jay – nature's 'Man from Porlock' – shatters a delicately spun line and jerks me out of the reverie for a few moments. But soon the balm returns and the images begin to dance, the words to trickle, once again, onto the page. I see the prison hospital, sense his boredom and frustration, the weeks and months caged up, losing weight – prepared to give anything to get out of this.

But then the wind in the trees changes and I am struck by an obvious yet vitally important thought: the humiliation of the whole thing. Soldiering of the type he endured depends upon pride, solidarity, comrades in arms fighting as much to defend one another as to take out the enemy. To be suddenly plucked out of that fraternal net, mutilated, disarmed and herded away to an uncertain fate at the point of an enemy gun must be a shattering experience. There's relief, perhaps, not to be dead, but still a deep humiliation, to be stripped of all pride, honour, comradeship, value. I never thought about this when he was alive, never talked to him about it. Yet it must have been the first great wound, the first great scar, the war inflicted on him.

In August 1943, the hand then considered healed, Dad

was transferred to an officers' POW camp just outside Modena. There he was recommended for repatriation. Events overtook him, however. On 8 September 1943 the Italians declared an armistice and pulled out of the war. By then the Allies had taken Sicily and made several landings in southern Italy. The Germans got wind of the Italian plan to pull out and had already largely occupied their ex-ally's country by the time its leaders declared its change of sides.

There was jubilation when the imprisoned officers heard the news and watched their Italian guards drop their guns and run off into the hills. With the Italians out, most thought the war in Italy would be over in a matter of weeks and they would all be free. But a lot of prisoners, preferring not to wait, hopped over the wall and disappeared. In all, about half of the 80,000 Allied POWs held in Italy absconded in the following days. In Dad's camp the SBO (Senior British Officer), in an act more typical of the First World War than the Second, called his men to the parade ground and advised them strongly against escaping, telling them to remain within the camp 'until the situation is brought properly under control'.

In the next two days there was much debate about whether to take the SBO's advice and sit tight, or to get out while the going was good. At the same time a more subtle process was at work. Many of the remaining prisoners were quietly forming little groups of two and three, planning to escape and go on the run together. Even though his wounded hand gave him a handicap, Dad was determined to join one of these groups.

*

That evening I took a walk with Tom Cokayne, a friend of Mark's. In the course of the conversation, I discovered that he too had wanted to get out at the last moment, but had been unable to find a congenial companion. Probably if we had met up at the time, we should be gone together. He was as angry as I was about missing such a heaven-sent choice. Tom was twenty-three, and looked even younger. He was slightly built; his hair, which had grown rather long, was fair; his skin, tanned brown by the sun, was fresh and clear. In spite of the gentleness of his manner and his not very tough frame, he struck me as a person who possessed plenty of quiet courage, and who would not lose his head in a crisis. He was also good company and had a pleasantly ironic sense of humour. I liked him a lot, but I did not know then how magnificently he would live up to that first impression which I had formed of him.

So Dad and Tom paired up and decided to get out together as soon as an opportunity arose. But by the next morning it was too late – the Germans arrived, took over the camp and announced that all prisoners would be transferred by train to Germany. Before the Germans gained proper control, Dad, Tom and a friend of Tom's called David Rollo decided to hide in the camp and avoid all roll calls. Their plan was to get away once the Germans had moved the more docile and obedient of their captives – including, of course, the SBO – to Germany.

Not surprisingly, a hell of a lot of other officers had the same idea, and there followed three days of nerve-racking games of hide-and-seek, with prisoners frantically trying to dig tunnels, or hide under mattresses, down drains, over lavatory cisterns – anywhere they wouldn't be counted. At one point Dad drew cards for a place in a stinking drain. He was both skilled and lucky with cards. He drew the ace of spades, while Tom drew only a three of hearts. Tom put the manhole cover over Dad and David then skulked off to find a hiding place for himself. A day later the drain had been nabbed by another pair, so Tom and Dad devised an ingenious hiding place.

I had noticed an immense pile of rubbish at the entrance to one of the bungalows. For want of a better place, we decided to secrete ourselves in the middle of it, until the others had been taken away, when we hoped to be able to emerge and mingle with the rear party. We had two lots of luggage, 'escape kit' as described, and stuff which we should need if we were discovered and taken to Germany. We took both lots over to the rubbish tip and buried them in an old packing case with rubbish heaped on top. Tom then scooped a large hole at the back of the heap. We secured two mattresses from the bungalow, one to lie on and the other to put over us. I crawled in between them, Tom piled rubbish on top, and, having enlisted a passer-by to complete the covering and camouflage, clambered in beside me.

It was stiflingly hot but otherwise not unbearable, thanks to the mattresses . . . All the Germans wore hobnailed boots, so that we got plenty of warning when any Jerries were approaching. (Most P.O.W.s wore shoes or sandals.) We had to suppress a tendency to giggle when anyone passed, or pitched something on top of us. We wondered whether the whole rubbish heap was heaving up and down with our breathing. Someone came and threw a lot of cold tea over my feet, but as he was wearing boots, and therefore might con-ceivably have been a Jerry, I was unable to voice a protest.

*We had sweltered in our unsavoury immersion for about
an hour when we heard footsteps, unmistakably German,
approaching. They stopped, two Jerries intent on plunder,
and started to rummage about in front of the heap. Our
blood pressure rose, as Damon Runyan puts it, 'to maybe a
million'. Fortunately, they became bored before they got far
enough to unearth us, and departed, probably in search of
more productive looting grounds.*

Eventually all the more docile and unlucky prisoners
were led away and the remaining Germans finished
looting the Red Cross parcels and abandoned POWs'
possessions. David called Tom and Dad out of the rubbish
pile, where they had lain for more than a day. The trio
skulked around until dark, as there were still a few prowling Germans in the camp. The perimeter wall lights
flashed on, then went off again. The escapers donned the
civilian clothes they had acquired from their Italian
guards. First a South African hauled himself up onto the
prison wall, cut a large hole in the wire and slipped away
to freedom.

It was the turn of Dad, Tom and David next.

*Tom climbed first, David and I making stirrups for his feet.
He made it look easy and sat astride the top, to give me a
hand up, whilst David shoved from behind. I tore a large
hole in the seat of my pink Italian trousers on a strand of
barbed wire but managed the one-handed climb with less
difficulty than I had feared.*

'Here, take this, can you?' said David, indicating the kit.

*For what seemed an age, I was perched on the top of the
wall, reaching down to take the stuff from David and*

passing it down to Tom on the other side – David's haversack and spare boots, my little attaché case, Tom's haversack, and the water bottle. At last everything was over and I could drop down the other side.

There was a hole cut in the outside fence. I got myself and the kit through, whilst Tom helped David over.

We were FREE!

We charged through a vineyard, grabbing bunches of grapes from above us as we went, and cheered on our way by a few excited Italians. At the end was a thick hedge with a grass path on the other side. We fought our way through the brambles. Standing on the path was an aged and bewhiskered Italian, evidently the smallholder. I was wondering whether he was about to take exception to this mad exodus through his vineyard and hedge when, 'Bravo! Bravo! Figlio mio!' he exclaimed, seized me in his arms and kissed me on both cheeks.

Knowing practically no Italian, I murmured appropriate noises, disengaged myself as gently as I could, and we were off again.

For the next few days the escapers were utterly high on their new-found freedom. Local people plied them with wine, bread and ham and they gorged themselves on grapes and tomatoes. The weather was fine and the going good.

Once safely away from the camp, they considered their options. They could head north and try to make it to neutral Switzerland, from where they could be repatriated. But this would entail crossing the Lombardy plain at a time when German troops were flooding across northern Italy. The alternative was to head south, towards the Allied bridgeheads. This looked like the best bet. Their first hurdle was the mountain barrier immediately in front of them: the Apennines.

My eyes scan the land but there is no movement, no-one out there, only the little puppet-soldiers dancing on the inside of my head. How to find them, how to bring about the meeting of minds that I seek, I don't know. Tomorrow, though, I'll have a first stab: I'll head high up into the Apennines and see if I can perhaps pick up their trail, catch their scent there.

Opening the front door to fetch the logs, I find that Marcello has silently left on the doorstep a bag of wild mushrooms, fresh from our woods today. I have a few spicy sausages from the village butcher in the fridge, so supper will be of the finest, before the odyssey begins.

CHAPTER THREE

14th September 1943

*Feeling ourselves out of the danger zone, we had time to look
round and appreciate our surroundings – the rich, fertile land,
the stalwart fruit trees with their inverted arches of clustering
vines, the cosy, homely-looking farmsteads, all bathed in the
warm yet not too hot sunshine of a late summer's afternoon.
There was no need to hurry. We were content to put a few
more miles between ourselves and the town, and were not
greatly bothered about our direction, provided we headed
roughly south. Tom's local map would take us to Vignola, a
village about fifteen miles away at the foothills of the Apennines.*

*Towards evening we decided to seek a night's lodging and
stopped at the next farmhouse. The family, a large one,
crowded round us, curious and somewhat reserved, the
women's brows creased in puzzled frowns, the children with
their mouths open.*

*'We are three English officers,' Tom explained with his
engaging smile.*

'Sono Inglesi ... scappati dai Tedeschi [*Germans*] ...
bene! bene!'

And then a spate of questions, a few of which Tom understood and did his best to answer.

Where did we come from? ... Where were we going? ... How old were we? ... What military class? (Too difficult to explain that there weren't military classes in England.) ... What rank were we? ... 'Un capitano e due tenenti'
... Who was the Capitano? *(I became the centre of interest.)* 'I was wounded? ... where was I wounded? ... When? ... Who by? ...' *The women fussed over my hand as if I were a favourite nephew.*

During a short lull, Tom asked one of the men if we might stay here the night 'on the straw'. Certainly we could. Chairs and bottles of wine materialised from nowhere. News of our presence spread rapidly round the neighbouring farms, and friends of the family drifted in to look at the Inglesi *and congratulate us on our lucky escape from the* Tedeschi. *It required no knowledge of Italian to see just how popular were Mussolini's ex-allies.* 'Shoot them all' *was the general verdict, or a hand passed blood-curdlingly across the throat. We were assured that there were no* Tedeschi *or* Fascisti *in the neighbourhood. After a few more glasses of wine, I found myself discoursing fluently in Italianised French – one added an 'e', or 'o', according to how it sounded – which everyone was far too polite not to understand.*

Over the next few days, as the escapers made their way towards the Apennines, the local people continued to ply them with food and wine – so much so that Dad remarks: *Escaping through enemy-occupied territory assumed the aspect of a glorified pub-crawl.*

Typically, Tom somehow acquired a local map. Though, at twenty-three, he was younger than Dad, who was twenty-eight, and a lieutenant, Tom seems to have been the best adapted, personality-wise, to the new escaper world they found themselves in. Over the following weeks he most often took the initiative, suggested the next course of action, solved the immediate problems facing the escapers. Since he also spoke the best Italian of the threesome, he took it upon himself to be the principal spokesman for them.

Tom's map guided them to a place called Vignola. From there a little-used road wound its way up a river valley, climbed steeply over the ridge of the Apennines, then dropped down sharply to the Arno plain below. Even though the Germans were making sporadic use of this back route to Florence, the escapers decided to risk hitch-hiking.

Presently, round the corner drove a crimson-coloured civilian lorry. To ensure that it was not driven by a German, we had to wait until it was almost abreast of us, before we leapt through the hedge and signalled the driver to halt. There were two men in the front and three small boys on top of the cargo in the back. The driver gladly consented to give us a lift: his destination was Montese, a village high up in the mountains, about a third of the way to Florence. David squeezed into the front, between the driver and his mate, whilst Tom and I clambered up on top.

The lorry was heavily loaded with a queer assortment of freight, varying from several big boxes of cheese to a pair of skis. As it chugged slowly into the hills a superb panorama of the Penaro valley stretched itself out beneath us – the white river bed, with its isolated pools, glittering silver in the sun; the rich, fertile plain gradually giving place to steep, terraced vineyards and rugged mountain peaks. The valley below looked prosperous and at peace, with its white, red-roofed farmhouses standing out brilliantly in the bright sunlight.

Everyone was happy and gay, the small boys overjoyed to help three British officers to escape from the hated Tedeschi. As for us, the novelty of freedom had not yet worn off. How lucky we were to be enjoying such a perfect day amidst such magnificent scenery, with every yard taking us nearer to real and lasting liberty!

As the gradient steepened, the lorry's speed dropped so low that the boys could take it in turns to leap off, grab a bunch of grapes, run after the lorry until they caught it up, and scramble on again. Every few miles the radiator boiled over, the lorry ground to a standstill, and one of the lads would be dispatched with a bucket to the nearest farm for water.

Up in the mountains the air was cool and invigorating. The old lorry seemed to appreciate it too, for downhill it lurched along at a princely 20 m.p.h., and the small boys had to be content with looting the boxes of cheese. Towards evening the driver drew up at a junction, where he advised us to get off. We thanked him for this invaluable lift and wished him God-speed.

At the farm, it rains heavily in the night, but by eight thirty in the morning it has stopped, leaving overcast skies, the air soggy and leaden. I set out on wet, slippery roads, but by the time I reach Florence, about an hour and a half's drive, they are dry. Banks of cloud still hang over the mountains to the north, shrouding many peaks. I check my map carefully and find a spot marked 'M. Vignola', on a mountain road heading south, which I assume the escapers took. Some way down the road there is the village of Montese, which I know they passed through. I can make it to M. Vignola by leaving the Florence–Bologna motorway at the little village of Sasso Marconi, just short of Bologna.

Within minutes I am high in the mountains. Some of the peaks are wooded; others just bare rock – crags, cliffs, scree faces and majestic solid pinnacles. The lower slopes and high valleys are given over to farming and forestry. Bursts of sunlight slip between the scudding clouds, playing on the deep greens of grass and trees, contrasting with the rich browns of ploughed land and the honey yellow of the rock faces. The leaves of the deciduous trees are just beginning to fall, frolicking on the breeze and sticking to the damp road surface.

As the road reaches the crest, it seems almost as if I am in Switzerland – alpine meadows, fruit orchards, woodland and rocky crags and peaks. Yet the whole area is densely settled. Villages every few kilometres are fringed by small warehouses and light-industrial 'units' – modern metallic sheds that scar the landscape but provide employment. In the areas between the villages there are plenty of farmhouses, though nearly all of them are closed up, with fences ringing them and signs reading 'Beware of the Dog', 'Private Property', 'Access Forbidden' and suchlike. These are now the weekend retreats of wealthy Bolognese and Florentines. In Dad's day they were all occupied by *contadini*, sharecropper families who were given the house and smallholding in return for half of their annual produce, paid to the landlord at harvest time. These were the people who constantly provided the escapers with food, drink and shelter.

As they travelled south, Dad, Tom and David were usually offered the hay of a farmer's manger as overnight beds, covered in old coats in the oxen stall. Many times one or other of them was woken by a rasping lick from one of their bovine stall-mates.

The *contadini* are mostly very poor, subsistence farmers. Every family keeps a pig or two, who are turned into crude ham, bacon, salami and sausages just before Christmas, and everyone conserves large supplies of fruit and vegetables, either in oil or by sun-drying, to sustain them through the winter months. In the 1940s few children had shoes and education was sparse, but most of the people I know who grew up in *contadini* families have warm memories of their childhood. At the very least there was always something good to eat, a cheerful fire to sit round and loving grandparents to care for them.

On my day's drive through the Apennines I come across only one *contadini*-style farmstead. Rounding a sharp bend, the road dips into a little hollow in the hillside and passes through the middle of the farmyard. I slow right down as chickens scatter before my wheels and an old dog barks hoarsely. A beautiful fresh hay rick, a tubular pile built up round a single vertical pole, is still being added to, by hand. Bits of rusty ploughs and rakes lie strewn round the yard, and two goats poke their heads out of the ground-floor windows of the house. White doves flutter among the roof tiles. Just the sort of place where the escapers would have sought, and been given, a meal or a place to sleep for the night.

Around midday I reach the crossroads where I think the lorry driver dropped my father, at the turn-off to Montese. Dad describes it in some detail but I can't make it fit, mostly because several new warehouses now dominate the junction. But there is a small bar-trattoria on the corner, so I sidle in and order a glass of wine. The place is empty but for a very tired-looking woman who serves me a sour, unpleasant red. As there is little point in making enquiries about a hitch-hiker who passed through here fifty-seven years ago, I set the glass down and leave. Before getting back in the car, I walk round a little, sniffing the place out. I notice a faint stirring in the pit of my stomach, a tingling in the upper back – nostalgia, I suppose it could be called, a haunting feeling.

The sign tells me Montese is only three kilometres away, so I might as well go down there. Who knows, maybe it's a quiet little place, with a bar and some old gaffers who might remember the family who had the only lorry in the village during the war.

No such luck. Montese is now almost a small town, with lots of new houses, yet more light industry on the fringes, but no bar. Now that the weather has turned, there is nobody about: not a soul to be seen. Besides, as it's siesta time, all the shops are shut and the folk would anyway be back at home, eating and resting.

As I pass through the village I see a large sign to Vignola, so I pull up to consult my map. There, close to Modena, is a town called Vignola, at the head of the valley that leads down to Montese. So I'd got this bit of their route wrong. They hadn't come up the road I was on this morning, they'd followed a different road further to the west. I drive down the hill to the correct junction where the first lorry driver dropped them.

Before I begin to follow their route through the mountains, the weather closes in completely. I can see the storm nestling at the top of the valley, a shroud of grey-black cloud, and I let the little hire car carry me right into it. Vertical sheets of water cascade from the sky, occasionally slanting diagonally as the wind bends them. The rain brings back a soaking Saturday afternoon in February, when I was about six years old.

While it was walks to the pub and war stories on Sunday, every Saturday from February to June we went to a point-to-point. This particular day it was at Kimble, just below the Chiltern escarpment. I and brother Simon were with Dad. The rain cascaded down as we ate our sandwiches and sipped hot soup in the car. Dad studied the form very seriously, and when he was ready we went through our race cards, marking up his selections for each race.

The rain showed no sign of relenting, so we donned wellingtons, macs and hats and piled out of the car. Simon decided to go and see the stream under the water jump, while Dad and I headed for the paddock to inspect the horses. There was a crowd there, so I let go of Dad's hand and slid between tweed-clad legs until I reached the rail. I could then look under it at the horses. A few moments later I turned to glance at Dad, but he was nowhere to be seen. He was so tall I could always easily see his head above everyone else's, but on this occasion it was definitely not there.

Fighting off panic, I wove my way out of the crowd, but still I couldn't see him. By then I was really scared. I shouted, 'Daddy, Daddy!' There was no reply. Tears started to well in my eyes. I shouted again, but still nothing. This time, though, a policeman came over and asked me what was the trouble. Then he told me to go with him.

I screamed that I didn't want to go with him, I just wanted my daddy. He took my hand and led me to the tent of the hunt secretary, who made an announcement over the tannoy that Captain Reid's small son was here to be collected.

Dad was livid, not because he was embarrassed by the public announcement, but because my disappearance interfered with the pressing routine of preparing his bets for the next race. He took me to join Simon and we were both instructed to play in the stream near the water jump and not to stray from there. I was hugely relieved Dad had found me, that he hadn't disappeared.

Despite the rain and getting lost, it was a wonderful day. Saturdays at the races always were, because Dad really enjoyed himself and he let us in on his act; we shared his pleasure. And he was certainly not to be put off by anything so banal as a lost boy or bad weather.

Back in the Apennines, I pass through a village confidently called Belvedere. There's no chance of seeing the beautiful view today, though. The road becomes an endless series of hairpin bends, with torrents of water pouring across the tarmac surface straight downwards.

Somewhere around here the escapers managed to ambush their second lorry, but there's little hope of finding the spot in this weather.

Before the astonished driver had time to realise what was happening, we had all three wedged ourselves in front, Tom explaining, apologising and entreating. While he was talking, the leading vehicle of a German convoy drove round the corner facing us. Inwardly we swore, but the driver was not

in the least disconcerted. Finding it impossible to manipulate
his gears with four people in front, he calmly got out and
unlocked the back door for David, whilst German trucks and
motorcycles streamed past. Not until he had got in and
started up did it occur to us to enquire his destination.

'Florence,' he told us.

'Florence!' Tom and I exclaimed together. In our most
optimistic moments we had not anticipated a lift the whole
way to the plains, let alone to Florence itself. We shouted the
glad news back to David.

The driver, a charming individual, was a citizen of
Bologna. He told us how bitterly the working classes hated
Fascism and how they had been working for its overthrow.
He hoped that Badoglio would declare war on Germany and
that the Germans would soon be driven out of Italy.

After the excursions and alarms of the last few days, it was
delightful to sit back, in the relative security of a lorry,
speeding south. There was still an unceasing flow of German
transport, northward bound, which Tom thought might be
from Corsica, recently evacuated by the enemy. Once we
were held up at a traffic block until a German soldier
signalled us through. We gave him a wave of acknowledge-
ment. He smiled and waved back. Tom laughed.

The driver dropped Dad, Tom and David on the outskirts of Florence, pressing a fifty-lire note into Dad's
hand and wishing them the best of luck. So they set off on
foot, intent on working their way round to the west and
south of the great city.

I cross their tracks roughly where I turn south to Siena,
on my way back to the farm in the evening. In many ways
it has been a disappointing day. Not only did I get the

route wrong part of the time, even when I was on the right track I didn't feel I was accomplishing anything more than a vicarious piece of patri-tourism. The rain didn't help, but all I managed to achieve were a few glimpses of the views they had seen, and briefly shared the same exhilaration at the dramatic scenery earlier in the day.

One negative aspect in particular struck me: I established in the space of a few hours that the human landscape the escapers moved through has now almost entirely vanished. Traditional *contadino* farmsteads have been converted wholesale into weekend retreats for the urban middle classes, sweeping away with them an entire lifestyle. The land itself is no longer the focus of rural people's occupation, being displaced now by tin and concrete boxes housing light industry on the fringes of every village and hamlet I passed through. I wonder if just following in Dad's footsteps will ever bring me closer to him.

Back at the farm, though, sitting on Dad's terrace, I admit to myself that the day's failures can't all be attributed to changes in the landscape. There is a more fundamental problem. In terms of empathy with the escapers' experiences, whizzing around in a car just checking out locations has no impact at all. I am no closer now to what they had been through physically or emotionally than I was when I set out this morning. I see now that I will somehow have to move closer to their time frame, their pace and rhythm, if I am going to make any progress. Luckily, the next major phase of their journey takes place largely on foot. Time to get out the walking shoes.

CHAPTER FOUR

BY THE TIME THE ESCAPERS WERE SKIRTING FLORENCE, they'd been on the run for about a week and a routine was emerging. They walked in the morning, stopped for a picnic of donated food or 'foraged' sweetcorn, tomatoes and grapes in the heat of the day, then walked on. At about four or five they started looking for somewhere to stay for the night. They knew that *contadino* farmhouses in remote spots were their best bet, but as they worked their way round Florence they found that the suburbs were mostly composed of large private villas, owned by people who were generally not overjoyed at the prospect of putting up bedraggled British POWs, even if they were officers.

Over a ridge, we came upon a small country road with three or four large residential houses lying back from it.

'Let's give them one more chance before we look for a farmhouse,' one of us suggested. 'If we try that one at the end it won't take us out of our way.'

In the front garden two men were working. Tom explained the usual: 'Three English officers, very tired . . .' The men seemed surprised. After a short conversation they called up to someone at one of the upstairs windows of the villa.

'One moment,' called a gruff voice from within.

A conversation ensued which we didn't understand. Then a large, black-haired, swarthy-looking fellow, dressed in riding breeches, appeared on the balcony.

'I'm a policeman, you know,' he announced, slowly descending the staircase.

We looked at each other, considering instant flight; but, since he didn't appear to be armed, we stood our ground. Smiling at our embarrassment, he came across and wrung us warmly by the hand. In a few words he bade us have no fear: he was not a Fascist, and he disliked the Tedeschi *as cordially as we did ourselves. Nor was he satisfied until we had promised to accept his hospitality for the night. Explaining that he wished us to remain concealed until after dark, he showed us to a loft above his garage.*

It turned out that our host was no ordinary policeman, but the chief Carabiniere *of the district. In fact, his was the one house we would have walked miles to avoid, had we known! He brought us a basket of figs, wine, and a tub of water to bath in. Rested and refreshed, we chatted together until the* Carabiniere *asked to be excused – there was a transmission from* Radio Londra *which he wished to hear. He promised that, after supper, we too might listen to the news.*

We were dozing when he returned, after dark, to escort us through to the house. He introduced us to his wife, who had prepared a sumptuous meal for us – soup, stew, and potatoes, dessert, red and white wine. On the potatoes was sprinkled something black, which I was surprised to discover was caviare.

'Dai nostri alliati Russi?' I asked my hostess with a smile.

The Carabiniere, *having heard our story, was anxious to know our plans for the future. When he learnt of our intention to hitch-hike on the Rome road, he advised us strongly against such a course. There were many more Germans down here, he told us, and few Italian lorries. Tom asked what he would recommend.*

'Go into the mountains and wait there a week or two, until your troops arrive.'

He named a village, Luca Lena, where we would be safe from Tedeschi, Fascisti *and* Carabinieri! *We promised to consider his suggestion.*

The next day they took his advice and hiked up into the Chianti hills.

The second night after their stay with the *carabiniere*, they called at a priest's house in the late afternoon. He arranged their accommodation and took supper with them. As the conversation turned to the state of the nation, the priest opened a handsome and detailed map of Italy. Throughout the evening the escapers dropped loud hints about how useful it would be for them, but the *padre* merely replied that he found it very helpful for following the news. The next morning, Tom decided to go and ask for the map point-blank.

I asked him if we could have it but he pretended not to understand. I was afraid, if I pressed him, he might refuse altogether, so I asked him if I could take it away and make a copy.

As he was speaking Tom spread it out on the ground. It was, of course, exactly what we needed. It showed all the villages, all the major roads and most of the minor ones. Three covetous pairs of eyes feasted themselves on its clear, shiny surface.

'We do need it much more than he does,' Tom said. We looked at it some more. At last I voiced what was in all our minds:

'We could find ourselves forced to leave very suddenly.'

David said: 'That's what I should do if I were alone.'

Tom and I laughed.

A few minutes later we were scrambling up the hillside away from the village – plus one map and three guilty consciences.

I don't know which road the escapers took from Florence to Lucolena, but they arrived there a couple of days later. To catch up with them, I decide to drive the hire car back to Pisa then take the train through Florence to a little station called Figline, in the Arno valley directly below Lucolena. I note with a little trepidation that Figline lies at 126 metres above sea level, whereas a point very close to Lucolena is marked at 554 metres. The distance is only about fifteen kilometres, but it is more than 400 metres up. I heft my pack and set off. It is early in the afternoon.

I soon clear the town. The first stretch is uphill all the way. There's not much traffic, but when lorries do pass they seem to take little notice of a toiling pedestrian. Several times I resort to evasive action by leaping into the ditch. The weather is good and the air clean when I'm not doused in diesel fumes. Much of the hillside is wooded, but I soon reach stretches of vineyards with verge-side notices proclaiming the wine to be Chianti Classico.

Stopping to drink water at an intersection I realize that, despite my best efforts to pare it down, my pack is still too heavy (it weighed in at eleven kilos at Gatwick and I have added my leather jacket to it since then). I have made the basic mistake of packing just one more than the bare minimum of trousers, socks, underwear, and little extras like a book or two. This has added the lethal two or three kilos which convert an easily manageable pack into a leaden burden under tough conditions – such as walking continually uphill.

An hour later I come to a junction. The road to Lucolena is to the left, rising steeply upwards. This is where the direct road from Florence meets the route I have taken from Figline. Now I am definitely following the path the escapers took. I am walking in their tracks. A burst of elation ripples through me, but is soon extinguished by the gradient. I set off up the hill, reasoning – praying – that it can't go on like this all the way to Lucolena. It can and does. Without a single let-up. Through dense woodland, round sharp bends, past a newly planted walnut grove with a surreal roadside notice that reads: 'Parasitic Treatment. Danger of Death. Do Not Enter'.

I try to take my mind off the climb by imagining what the road would really have been like fifty years ago. Would it have been paved? I doubt it, since it leads only to a little rural backwater. Even today there are still hundreds of miles of dirt tracks linking small villages, hamlets and isolated farms throughout Italy.

Increasingly sore feet further slow my progress, but

finally I reach the terraced vineyards below Lucolena. It is six o'clock and gaggles of men are strolling out of the vineyards, many carrying plastic bags containing a few bunches of grapes. The harvest is evidently late at this altitude. The men look as tired as I am, having spent the day bent over the vines, snipping bunches and tossing them into baskets on their backs. I ask one group if they know of a place to stay, but, shrugging their shoulders, they explain that they are not from around here. Migrant labour, seasonal pickers from Italy's still-poor deep south, judging by their accents. One hands me a bunch of grapes; another calls to a 'local' to advise me.

I trudge on wearily up the hill and come to a roadside sign to an *agriturismo*, offering chalets and apartments, 1,500 metres away. Fifteen hundred metres, a twenty-minute walk, and no guarantee it would be open. I plod on towards the village.

It's something of a curse for walkers that for at least the last two and a half thousand years the Etruscans, Romans, Florentines, Sienese and the rest have all preferred to build their villages and towns atop the highest hills they could find. Very picturesque, of course, and away from the mosquitoes in the valleys. Good for defence and fortification too, which is undoubtedly why the practice developed in the first place. From the dawn of time right up to a century ago there was an almost perpetual state of feud between the neighbouring states of Florence and Siena, on whose disputed frontiers I now stand. They plumped for the safety of the hilltops, and never mind the weariness of trudging home after a long day on the land or a visit to a neighbouring village. Living on high was not convenient when it came to water supplies either, a state of affairs that perhaps contributed to Aldous Huxley's immortal caricature of Italy as 'over-monumented and under-bathroomed'.

I keep climbing until I reach the walls of the village. The road runs in a curve below them, denying me access to the place itself. But from here I can look right down to the valley floor and Figline, from where I set out three hours ago. Now it's just a tiny speck far, far away in a vast panorama of hills and valleys.

Rounding a bend I come to a break in the wall, which opens out into a wide piazza with a bar at one end. As usual, a couple of old boys are sitting on benches outside the bar, chatting animatedly. I order a cold beer – ah, what bliss! – and ask if there are any rooms available to rent in the village. Nothing. I shudder.

'There's an *albergo* further up the hill, just out of the village. They have rooms, but I don't know if they're still open. It's only half a kilometre away,' the barman tells me.

I ask next if there is still a bridge in the village. This arouses his curiosity and I explain that my father was here in the war, that he sat on the bridge watching the pretty girls of Lucolena pass by. 'You won't see pretty girls from it now. There aren't any left in this village,' he mutters.

As the light is beginning to fade I decide to leave the bridge until later and stagger off uphill, praying that the *albergo* is open. The climb seems even steeper than the long ascent that afternoon and my feet scream at me. My calves, thighs and lower back are all aching too. But after a little over a kilometre I pass the village cemetery (always the last marker on the road out of a Tuscan village), round a bend and see the *albergo* sign in front of me. And, yes, it is open; and, yes, they do have a room; and, yes, the restaurant will be open from seven thirty until ten. Thank God.

Tom, David and Dad reached Lucolena on 22 September 1943. I make it here, on foot like them, fifty-seven years and twenty-six days later. Knowing that I am now following precisely their footsteps up these mountains makes the trail feel decidedly warmer.

CHAPTER FIVE

AROUND EIGHT O'CLOCK I HOBBLE OVER TO THE restaurant, shod in sandals and socks – only the British would dare! I expect the place to be empty, but no: at the table opposite me three large, jovial Germans are chatting loudly. When the waitress comes to take their order they ask her in broken English for a half litre of red wine. She stares back at them blankly. They look appealingly to me:

'*Mezzo litro di vino rosso, per favore,*' I translate.

'*Oh, ja, ja, danke. Mezzo litro di vino rosso, danke schön.*' They seem to find this very funny, and raise their glasses to salute me, then return to their noisy chat. The waitress takes my order from the menu and a little later a young Italian couple arrive. They are not offered a menu. Instead the *padrone* himself comes to their table, reels off a half-dozen dishes, then strongly recommends them to choose such-and-such, freshly made with the finest ingredients. This is the correct way to be served in Italy, but it does require a sophisticated grasp of the language and some knowledge of the local cuisine, of neither of which are we foreigners judged capable.

Shortly before I finish my meal six more people arrive and take the table next to me. Their conversation is less boisterous than the Germans'; they seem a little nervous, unsure of both language and food. I can't make out their speech, though I think it might be Central European. They wear smart clothes and gold jewellery, expensive shoes. As I leave I meet the *padrone* in the hall, and I ask him where they are from. 'Israelis,' he says: 'tourists from Israel.'

Dad's first active posting in the army was to the British Mandate of Palestine in 1936. Two privates in his platoon were shot dead by 'terrorists' on their first day there. By 1943 he was in full battle against the Nazi enemy, a war fought at least in part to halt the extermination of the Jews. And now here I am, in a restaurant in a remote corner of Italy, with all these deadly enemies rubbing shoulders, breaking bread just a few feet apart, less than sixty years after we had all been hell bent on tearing one another to pieces.

The next morning brings a sapphire sky of dazzling brilliance. The valleys below are filled with puffy mists, but up in our eyrie above the clouds the light shines like crystal.

Outside my room is a series of small outhouses. An old man stands at the door of one of them, pinkish-purple stalks and grape skins round his feet. He greets me heartily, introducing himself as Giuseppe.

'*Piacere. Sono Osvaldo.*' As there is no direct translation for Howard in Italian I was rechristened Oswald there a few days after I arrived in 1970.

Blackish juice trickles from the open lip at the bottom of Giuseppe's wine press. I enquire of this year's harvest and he assures me, as everyone has, that the millennial wine is very good, *speciale*. Not too many grapes but a very fine dry growing season, giving a mature harvest with plenty of sugar. Glancing round his *cantina*, chatting about his grape varieties, I can see that he is making his wine in the traditional way, in open vats.

Having run off the pure juice from the vat, he gently shovels the remaining mush into his press, to squeeze the last precious drops from it. The sale of wine made in this way is now illegal, unless it is carried out on an immense scale, using stainless-steel vats, clean tiled cellars with temperature control, and a plethora of other ludicrous EU regulations. It's a source of great rage to all the small makers of wine, oil and other traditional products in Italy, that the Euro-superstate seems determined to outlaw methods of production which have been handed down for countless generations. People are proud of the way they make their wine. They supply their families, friends and dependants living in the cities with the fruits of their labour. Many of these people come to help with the harvesting and making of wine and oil. The whole process is part and parcel of the fabric of life in Italy, binding people together. Yet nowadays the sleek bureaucrats of Brussels consider this type of tradition unhygienic, uneconomic, unjustifiable, and certainly not commercially viable.

Not that any of this much bothers old Giuseppe, who passes me a small glass of cloudy dark-pink liquid to admire and taste. I savour sweetness tinged with the yeasty tang of the first fermentation. It immediately reminds me of Dad's home-made wines.

As a boy, I spent a lot of the summer and autumn in fruit trees. In June and July it was the huge Morello cherry tree and the three Victoria plum trees. I passed the full baskets down to Dad, who acted as spotter, directing me where to scramble to next, making sure we got the best of the harvest before the wind shook the fruit free. With the cherries we made cherry ale, by adding beer and sugar to the mashed fruit. We left the mush in big bowls for a few days, then strained off the liquid into gallon glass jars, which Dad set by the Aga. There it bubbled steadily for months, and when it stopped we kids had great fun washing glass bottles while Dad boiled a pan full of corks, to soften and sterilize them. Then came the tasting. Dad would pick up the jar with his left hand and tip a tot into our special tasting glass. We took it in turns to sip. As most of the wines we made were slightly sweet, we kids smacked our lips with pleasure and pestered Dad for a second tot. He would chortle and concede, murmuring that we mustn't tell Mum he'd given us more, or he'd be for it. Cherry ale, plum sherry, elderflower champagne and elderberry wine, apple wine, damson wine – with Dad we scoured the countryside in search of wine-making fruits, flowers and berries. And in that first taste, at the end of the fermentation, there was always a yeasty tang, just like old Giuseppe's new vintage has.

I stroll down the hill to Lucolena to buy lunch at the grocer's shop, and find the bridge where Dad, Tom and David paused on their way through the village. In those days it must have been the uppermost access point to the village, controlling the route southwards. Sixty years ago I would have had to cross it, as Dad had done on his way south. But since the war the bypass road was built, converting this corner of the village into a backwater. No pretty girls to be seen here now, just a friendly, bustling nun, who gives me a quizzical look then returns to her conversation with two elderly residents. Little point in asking them if they recall a trio of dubious-looking strangers eyeing them up from the bridge fifty-seven years ago, I think.

The *alimentari* (grocery) in the square provides fresh bread, *salami toscana* and a few tomatoes for lunch.

Back at the *albergo* the old boy is collecting the last drops from his press.

'*Signore* Giuseppe, do you remember the time of the war, the time of the Armistice, when many Allied prisoners escaped?'

'I was only a boy at the time. I don't remember it very well, but I do remember Allied prisoners coming through here. Some even slept in the village, and more stayed at my uncle's farm up the valley. A few were still in their army uniforms, so we gave them clothes, old hats, and we fixed their boots if they were bad.'

This chance remark stops me in my tracks. It was just beyond Lucolena that the escapers met the young industrialist who was so keen to get a note from them.

The boss went on to explain how dangerous it was to help P.O.W.s. Otherwise he would have great pleasure in inviting us to his house. But we would understand that he was too well known here, that his house was too near the road for him to take such a risk. If, however, there was anything more we wanted ...?

Both Tom's and David's shoes were in a shocking state.

*Would there be any chance of getting them repaired? The
chauffeur was at once dispatched for the village shoemaker,
who presented himself a few minutes later. An obliging old
man, he promised to have them ready by the first thing in the
morning.*

*Having made our adieus, we took our leave. For Tom and
David in their stockinged feet, the walk back to the farm was
somewhat painful.*

*The cobbler was as good as his word. Before we had risen,
he brought the shoes, excellently repaired, and refused any
payment other than a few English cigarettes.*

'Did you know the village cobbler during the war,
Giuseppe?' I ask.

'Village cobbler? Sure. That was Uncle Aldo. He fixed
everyone's shoes in the war, even though he was old by
then. *Molto bravo, zio Aldo, molto bravo* . . . He died soon
after the war, but he always fixed our shoes for nothing.'

First contact. Giuseppe's uncle Aldo fixed Tom's and
David's shoes, almost for certain. For a moment I feel like
hugging the old man. Instead I tell him that Dad's friends'
shoes were repaired while they were here. Giuseppe nods
and smiles, sure that it would have been Uncle Aldo's
work.

'Were you afraid of the Germans, that they would be
angry if they found escaped prisoners with you?'

'We were very scared of them. They did kill some boys,
Italian boys from a village below here, because they found
prisoners in their houses; but they didn't come here much,
except at this time of year, to steal our wine.'

'My father remembered the bridge in the village. He
saw pretty girls there.'

'Yes. There were pretty girls here then. Some of them were sent up here to keep them safe from the soldiers in the city. Well, it obviously worked out OK for your father in the end, as here you are!'

I ask him rather gingerly about the road ahead.

'It's a good road, very smooth, with new asphalt all the way [my map marks it as being still partly a dirt road]. It climbs at first for a while, then it is downhill all the way to Radda in Chianti. It's not far at all – you'll easily make it there today. No, not twenty kilometres: fifteen at the most. Take your time, go slowly, rest often. It's beautiful countryside up there – enjoy yourself.'

Fortified with his advice I return to my room and heft my down-sized pack – I decided to abandon all surplus clothes and a couple of books last night – and step out. As I pass the old man at his press he waves gaily and calls out, *'Piano, piano!'* 'Gently does it!' I'm sure his uncle said exactly the same thing to the escapers. Though the *carabiniere* advised them to stay and wait it out in Lucolena, in fact they kept going through the Chianti mountains, taking their time but moving steadily southwards.

From the albergo the road climbs steadily a further hundred and fifty metres, round the east side of Monte San Michele – at 893 metres, the tallest peak in the Chianti mountains. After a couple of kilometres it cuts through a very grand estate with stone gates, a Palladian mansion and formal gardens with box hedges, all enclosed by a fearsome barbed-wire fence. It is marked every few metres with metal signs saying: 'PRIVATE PROPERTY. ACCESS FORBIDDEN. Intruders will be reported under local act no. [such-and-such].' I wonder idly if this is the estate of the keen young industrialist who got Uncle Aldo to fix the escapers' shoes.

Beyond the sizeable manor farm the fields gradually give way to woodland. Soon I enter a sort of 'profound dull tunnel', where each side of the road is eerily darkened by immense pine trees, their canopies so dense that nothing grows beneath them. At the top of this tunnel there is a shaft of light. Could it be the crest, the end of this eternal uphill passage?

It is indeed. The ground falls away and opens out into scrubby heathland, locally called *macchia*, with the road meandering southwards through it.

On taking out my map I can see that in the last twenty-four hours I have made a lot of ground. Dad, Tom and David reached Lucolena from Florence in about three days. As they ambled on, Dad estimated that they were covering about ten miles a day. It must have been around here that the escapers learned that you really can cover a lot of ground on foot if you want to and if you're lightly equipped. Italy is not a huge country. Even though the going over the mountains might be tough, Rome is less than two hundred miles away, reachable in twenty days without any great strain. The escapers allowed themselves about a month, a pretty realistic estimate. And apart from the odd fright, life, it seems, was sweet.

The first few days of freedom were idyllic. After several months in a prison camp, or – as in my case – a P.O.W. hospital, how can I give an adequate description of the joys of sudden liberty? Ever-changing loveliness of scenery; sweet country smells and the pungent aroma of the farmyard; fresh, wholesome food; the recurrent halts for wine; a sense of peace and goodwill inspired by the peasant people. And these incredible grapes: I should never have believed so many were grown in the whole world. At the rate of twelve bunches a day – a conservative estimate – I must already have consumed something like two hundred bunches!

From our day-to-day existence we have developed some sort of system. David carries my small suitcase, which I should find difficult with one hand. I carry his blanket pack, nominally secured by a safety pin, but woefully apt to fall to pieces at the most awkward moments. Tom has his own pack and the water bottle. I have lately had to insist on a reorganisation of luggage. David, our cook and quarter-master, is thoughtful and likes to look ahead. Consequently, when we pass a tomato patch he is in the habit of picking tomatoes (while Tom and I are eating them) and putting the ripest ones in the suitcase, where they squash all over my socks and washing things. Now I carry all the clothes in his pack and we use the suitcase for food only. Nobody objects to a slightly tomatoey piece of chocolate.

Sleeping à trois has its difficulties, especially if there is only one blanket. Generally, early in the night a furious struggle ensues between the two outside berths. Around 2 a.m. one is apt to wake up shivering, to find oneself completely uncovered. 'In the middle' is certainly the warmest, but one gets butted by knees and elbows in the stomach as well as in the small of the back. To economise on blades, we only shave every three or four days. We usually manage a daily wash.

For these first few days, the fact that we were escaping through enemy-occupied territory only added a spice to the novelty and joy of freedom. Now the tempo is increasing and the adventure is becoming more serious. To rejoin our forces

is the primary objective, to be attained at all costs, and the
sooner the better.

On the crest of the hill where I rest, all is utter peace until a pair of gunshots ring out. A flock of startled songbirds bounce into the sky and drift away down wind. It is hard to tell if the intrepid hunters were aiming at them – Italian *cacciatori* will shoot anything that moves – or whether the reports simply scared the birds into the air. One reason why there is so much hunting in Italy today is that Mussolini changed the trespass laws to open up private property to the *cacciatore*. His aim was to enrich the martial ardour of the nation. Half a century later few of these laws have been repealed and several million small songbirds, as well as larger game, are still sacrificed on the altar of *Il Duce*'s martial prowess every year.

By now I am well within the beautiful mountains Dad described before dropping down into 'the Chianti country'. Above the maximum altitude for grapes or olives, once more the landscape has an Alpine feel to it, like the high Apennine pastures I drove through a few days ago. The air is cool, almost cold, and damp. The sky is heavily overcast. Dew coats the pastures. Scrubby woodland covers much of the ground, occasionally broken by steep cliffs and rock faces. A drainage ditch runs down the side of the road, its soft mud pock-marked with the tracks of *cinghiali*, wild boar. These are the true objects of the hunters' desire. Italy teems with them – so much so that in some parts they are pests and a menace to agriculture.

Wild boar are clever animals; they seem to be able to read the signs on the trees that say 'No Hunting. Zone of repopulation and capture', and congregate there. Unfortunately humans are both clever and devious: every few years they suddenly re-label the trees, declassifying the sanctuary and allowing hunting to recommence. Many pigs die before they learn the escape routes to the newly designated safe areas.

As I climb what I hope is the final pass through the mountains, the hunting signs change, announcing '*Hacienda agricola d'Albola*', followed by 'Hunting only by arrangement with the management'. A few minutes later I stand at the top of a long, deep valley. I have crossed the watershed into the Chianti country proper.

As it widens, the Val d'Albola becomes steadily lusher, full to bursting with vineyards. Here the grapes are already picked, but the vines have not yet been pruned of last year's shoots. Their leaves are gradually burnishing as autumn stems the sap flow. A series of large and elegant buildings come into sight, all built in sandy-grey stone. Some are castle-like, with towers and battlements; others are more prosaic – large farms originally housing the land agents, farm managers and workers, I suspect.

I ease off my pack, pull out bread and Tuscan salami, and follow the old man's advice to take it easy. The air is chilly, but when the sun appears between the clouds its rays pierce right through my shirt to my back. A couple of mouthfuls of red wine from a small plastic bottle stashed in my pack mingle with the salami so perfectly that the moment seems sublime. I can of course savour to the full simple, beautiful things such as these. After all there is nobody, except perhaps a self-imposed phantom or two, chasing me.

Moments like these make poignant the central irony

facing the escapers. Dad, Tom and David soon found that they had stumbled into a veritable Arcadia. In sublime weather and glorious countryside, their 'escape' became a pleasant, if unusual, hiking holiday, with the added spice of a stimulating but limited element of risk. Even some of the bad guys, such as the *carabiniere* boss, turned out to be goodies. Much of the time it must have been hard to keep in mind the notion that there were in fact a lot of real bad guys out there, who could further their own ends by killing or capturing the escapers.

As the road carries me down into the valley proper, I notice that all the houses are in immaculate condition – new shutters, clean gravel, gardener-manicured lawns and rose bushes. In front stand Mercedes and BMWs, most sporting discreet but telltale 'D' stickers on their backsides. One of these pulls up at a house and, just as I pass, disgorges a large blonde lady from the back. She smiles broadly and offers a friendly *'Buon giorno'*. A school bus trundles up the hill, fondly delivers a single child to the large house beside the castle, then rolls back past me, down the hill.

It is all very peaceful, idyllic and almost totally deserted. Apart from the German lady and the child I see no one near the road all that day. No trace, either, of any more ramshackle, self-sustaining farmsteads. No small vegetable patches, barns, stacks of wood or hay, scattered ploughs and seed drills in the farmyard: nothing remotely resembling the smallholdings of the *contadini* who looked after the escapers so well as they passed through this valley half a century ago.

Just as old Giuseppe had insisted I would, I easily make it to Radda in Chianti that evening. I take a room in the old town. It is expensive, but large and airy, with a pleasant little terrace at rooftop level. Cooling my feet on the bare tiles, I listen to the evening settle over the town. Later I buy a bottle of the best Chianti Classico of the Val d'Albola, to taste the fruit of the land I have walked through today. Though good, it is not a great wine. On a whim I phone some distant acquaintances, Matthew and Maro Spender, who live a few kilometres to the south, just off the road I plan to take tomorrow. Maro immediately invites me to spend the next night with them. Back in my room I settle down with a glass of the Classico and reread the section of Dad's book covering this part of the journey.

The trail of the escapers is more hazy at this stage than at any other time. They continue to travel south through 'the Chianti country' for several more days, though bad weather both slows them down and makes them determined to get out of the mountains before the winter proper sets in. Somewhere in the hills Dad finds time to set down his reflections on their first two weeks on the run.

To us the most striking feature of this last fortnight has been the extraordinary friendliness of the vast majority of Italians. Even before the fall of Mussolini there was ample evidence that the people were war-weary and anti-Fascist. But we were not prepared for this overwhelming generosity and kindness. Every day someone goes out of his way to help us.

Nor can one attribute this general attitude to ulterior motives or a desire to 'get on the right side'. At every house where we have stayed we have insisted on leaving a note to our forces, informing them of the fact and asking that some recompense should be made. But only once have we been asked to do so, and in many instances the family has been reluctant to accept anything. As one padrone, whom Tom needed all his tact not to offend, remarked: 'We do this from our hearts, not because we expect anything in return.'

Their hospitality is the more remarkable for two reasons. Firstly, they are terrified of the Germans and are convinced, perhaps justifiably, that were they discovered harbouring us, or even rendering us assistance, they would be shot. [Though Dad apparently didn't know this, the Germans had indeed issued such an edict.] Secondly, setting aside the anti-British propaganda which has been pumped into them for the last eight years, Italy has suffered severely at the hands of the Allies. Her towns have been knocked to pieces by our air forces and she has incurred enormous losses on the field of battle. At almost every household we are told, without rancour, of relatives killed, wounded, or prisoner in Allied hands. The contadini depend, often for their very existence, on the labour of their sons. Yet only on that first morning after our escape has it ever been suggested that we might stay and earn our keep. And this grape-picking time is one of the busiest of the year. It has not been necessary to point out that their misfortunes are the fault of Mussolini and his disastrous policy of aggression, not of an enemy whom they have never learnt to hate.

Most of the young men we have met hail us as comrades in a common adventure, with the remark: 'I too have escaped.' Their 'escapes' have, however, been somewhat simpler than ours. All most of them had to do after the Armistice was to throw away their arms, borrow civilian clothes from local friends, and take the first train home. We have heard stories that some were arrested by Germans or Fascists and carted off as slave labour to Germany.

72

At eight o'clock the next morning church bells rouse all and sundry, exhorting the faithful to mass, drubbing the rest of us out of bed. I tumble out onto the roof terrace. The weather is perfect: the sun warm but not threatening, the air fresh and constantly stirred by little breezes.

I mull over the map a bit and catch up on my notes, spinning a little cocoon of then and now, cemented with sunshine. 'Writer's cocoon' is something I am familiar with, ever since my two-year sojourn in Amazonia. There I kept a daily diary and always set aside an hour or so to keep it up-to-date. I also wrote long, leisurely letters to friends and family at home. It was there I discovered that the act of writing can in itself be a form of escape, a release from the stress and bustle of everyday life. Rereading Dad's '*Diary Reflections, October 1943*' and writing my own, on 20 October 2000, I have little doubt where I inherited that trait from.

At eleven thirty my reverie is shattered by a sharp rapping on the door. The landlady insists that room-vacating time is eleven o'clock and she has to make the bed up, so I should get going *pronto*. Ten minutes later I am on the road.

It was somewhere in Chianti that the escapers first encountered *briscola*, an enigmatic card game played with a special pack according to rules intelligible only to the initiated. The passion of most elderly men in rural Italy, it is played with much gusto, mostly in the afternoons on tables in front of the local bar or trattoria. This was the game the old men were playing when we stopped in the village after the flood washed away the motorway, when I was thirteen. After the priest had arranged our lodgings for the evening, Dad took me back to the card table to watch. He stood chortling and muttering *'Dio buono'* – 'Good God' – as the game unfolded. With his keen gambling instincts, Dad was a good card player, but he was completely dumbfounded on his first encounter with *briscola*.

They dealt anticlockwise, from the bottom of the pack. Tom and I, intrigued, drew our chairs closer. The cards were different from English ones, the four suits being represented by logs, swords, money and jars. On closer inspection we noted that the kings and jacks were depicted as women and that the queens wore moustaches: there was also an extra court card, a gentleman on a horse. The play was anarchic. Nobody followed suit. The first trick would be taken by the ace of logs, the second by the two of money, the third by the horseman of jars, and the fourth by the three of swords, which, for some unknown reason, beat the king. The partners chatted to each other quite openly and swapped hands whenever they felt like it.

'We haven't dropped into a chapter of Alice in Wonderland *by any chance, have we?' I asked Tom.*

'Well, it can't be the vermouth, because we haven't had enough.'

I am looking forward to a rest and a cool beer in a similar setting, confidently expecting to find a game of *briscola* in the next village on my route, a small place called Lecchi. But this is not to be, in the heart of modern Chiantishire. The only bar is decidedly up-market. It is offering Chianti Classico 'to taste' at 5,000 lire (about £1.65) a glass. My local bar in southern Tuscany does a glass of good red wine for 500 lire. The barman, dressed like a Californian in Gucci shoes, Chinos with fancy belt and designer tennis shirt, has no Italian beer, just Beck's. Outside, in place of the expected *briscola* players, sit an elegant German couple, sipping the 'wine of the day' and nibbling *crostini*. A little later the barman appears outside, takes their order, then reappears with three cases of the Classico, which he loads into the back of his guests' Mercedes.

I reach Matthew's and Maro's house sooner than I expect. Matthew, a sculptor, is working energetically with an electric grinder, which bites at a gorgeous snow-white block of marble. He is covered from head to toe in white dust, a tall ghostly apparition with the burning eyes of a man in deep concentration. We talk briefly, but it is only five in the afternoon and I can see that Maro, who is a painter, is as keen to get back to her brushes as Matthew is to grind on. I retire to my notes on the terrace, where the members of the Spenders' family of peacocks are settling down to roost for the night.

Later, as he builds up a dancing wood fire in the open hearth, I explain to Matthew, as well as I can, what I am doing. He smirks and mutters: 'Filial piety, eh? Not something that would have sent me off hiking all over the place. My father rarely walked more than a few yards in his entire life!' His father was the poet Stephen Spender.

We talk of the war. Matthew's take on the confusing period 1943–4 is that both sides, Germans and Allies, looked on the conflict in Italy as conventional war and wished to fight it out by the rules. But neither the neutral Italian civilian population nor the escaped Allied POWs fitted into the conventional package; they were an unnecessary complication. So when they got in the way they got hit. Maro, concocting a superb mutton and vegetable broth in the kitchen, interjects that the Germans were much more callous than the Allies, they massacred Italian civilians all over the place. This is certainly true, but Matthew maintains that they weren't hell-bent on their extermination, as they were with the Jews, Russians, Gypsies and Poles. For the Germans, escaped POWs were like mosquitoes: swat them if you can, but otherwise take little notice.

The conversation meanders on to our own roles as parents and the bewildering transmission of character traits from one generation to the next. Maro points out that sometimes these traits skip a generation. Poor Matthew, she explains, has lived two-thirds of his life in terror of his domineering mother, and now their second daughter, Cosima, has inherited her grandmother's fiery temper. A little later the phone rings. It is Cosima, calling from London. Her father chats warmly to her for some time. She is passionately committed to the making of observational documentary films, a career her parents evidently approve of. As I have spent much of the last twenty years making factual films, we discussed earlier in the evening the great difficulties she faces. When Matthew tells her I am here, her immediate response is: 'Hah, I trust you're telling *him* how to make documentary films too, Dad.' Ouch!

In the morning we talk of my route. From somewhere round here the escapers got a lift in a van, which took them almost to Chiusi, more than fifty miles away. I have noticed on my map that there is a little country railway line running from Siena to Chiusi and I wonder if this train journey might be a pleasant way to cover the ground. Maro looks doubtful; she thinks the service has closed down. The simplest way to find out is evidently to walk down and see for myself. The closest intersection with the railway line is about twenty kilometres away. Matthew talks me through the nicest route south, along several dirt roads, and I bid them farewell.

The walk is uneventful, some of it through the dramatic terrain known as *Le Crete Sinese*, the Sienese moorlands. Here the heavy clay soils are ploughed following the contours, the earths an array of yellows, browns and greys. Single farmhouses and cypresses dot the horizons like stark sentinels. By mid-afternoon I am out of the *Crete* and approaching the railway line. As I cross a bridge over it, I can see the rails gleaming, so I know the track is still in use. On the other side there is a bar, a friendly little place with plenty of local people coming and going. The landlord tells me that the train is still running, but it can only be taken from Siena. A bus to the town will be passing the bar in ten minutes' time. I know I am drifting from my target, that the escapers are totally out of sight. But at times, alone and on foot, you have to let circumstances carry you, 'go with the flow', and trust you'll reconnect with the purpose, the mission, some time in the future.

I take a room in the Hotel Toscana, in the centre of Siena, just behind the Piazza del Campo, the open 'field' where *il Palio*, the famous horserace, is run. From the window I can see the side of the massive tower that dominates the *campo*, and hear its bells.

As I am stripping off my walking clothes a sound drifts up to me which you can hear only in Siena. Massive rolls on snare drums cut through the air in a marching beat.

Snap, snap, snap-snap-snap ... snap, snap, snap-snap-snap. Then come the voices, the primordial cries of young, exultant males, half-shouting, half-singing, all testosterone, rising to a searing roar of defiant victory.

CHAPTER SIX

THE WAR-CRIES FROM THE PARADE BELOW MUST SURELY be connected with Siena's celebrated *Palio*, but the timing seems all wrong. The races are run in July and August, and, though the festivities go on for a month or more afterwards, all should have been done and dusted by now, late in October. It turns out, though, that this year a special millennial third race has been run in September and what is going on now is the parade of the victorious district – *Selva*, the forest. The coming of the twenty-first century has evidently provided a good enough excuse for the Sienese to extend the battle season for an extra month.

Siena is a spectacularly beautiful city, full of glorious buildings and art treasures. It is the only place in the world where until very recently the main public hospital was adorned with Renaissance frescos of medical treatments. You could lie in bed with your drip and monitor alongside and see on the walls exactly how you would have been treated five centuries previously.

The *Palio* is the jewel in the city's crown, an

extraordinarily colourful and exhilarating pageant, played out with such elaborate ritual that it's easy to think the whole thing has been cooked up as a tourist attraction. Nothing could be further from the truth. Matthew Spender's daughter Cosima was documenting the *Palio* season on video the first time I visited their house, and she told me what really goes on. For the Sienese the *Palio* is all. Tourists are about as relevant as the flies that pester the racehorses' eyes and flanks. In this world there is only black and white: the brothers and sisters within; the enemy without. It is the original gladiatorial circus, the Renaissance football crowd, in full cry for days, weeks, on end, reaching fever pitch again and again.

Each *contrada* has one specific rival or more and the contest is as much about beating your individual enemy as winning the race over all. The most famous adversarial pair are the *Onda* (wave) and *Torre* (tower), who literally hate each other with a vengeance.

After the races, losing jockeys (who are traditionally Sardinian and therefore untrustworthy, liable to take bribes) are torn from their horses and beaten mercilessly. Those who are unlucky enough to fall – a common misfortune, as they hurtle bareback around the U-bends of the circuit at 50 kph – receive the same battering. These occurrences have been recorded by TV cameras and nobody gives a toss. This is a Sienese *contrada* matter and the rest of the world can get lost ... It's a deep, dark, murky world where hatred, vengeance and humiliation go hand in hand with pride, glory and jubilation.

I lie with my window open, listening to the baying of the packs. The battle here is not between rival dukedoms or city states, but between neighbouring districts of just one town. Though it doesn't result in slaughter, all the emotions associated with warfare are brought to play during the *Palio*. You can almost feel the adrenalin coursing through the streets. The climactic cavalry charge unleashes ecstasy for the lucky few and misery for the losers, but at least half of the population's honour is upheld by the defeat of their own *contrada*'s principal enemy.

With the cries echoing up from below I am experiencing an aspect of the Italian psyche that is not so apparent under normal conditions. Generation after generation have thrived over the centuries in almost continual states of political and military turmoil, so now every Italian is aware of belonging to a complex network of loyalties. Within the Sienese walls you are a member of *contrada* X, and thus a sworn enemy of *contrada* Y. Outside the walls you are a Sienese, a deadly enemy of all Florentines. But then you and the Florentines are also Tuscans, all pitting your wits against the Vatican, Genoa, Venice or Milan. And you remain aware of other rival, even enemy, networks close at hand, some perhaps lurking in the shadows, biding their time. They must all be dealt with on a daily basis. The Armistice of 1943 upset the apple cart of the Fascist *status quo* and forced everyone to redefine their allegiances and animosities. This process was complicated enormously by the presence of two large foreign armies at the heart of the motherland, forty thousand foreigners on the run and a bewildering plethora of local political alignments, from Socialists and Communists, resistance fighters and local militias to the armed remnants of Fascist authority. It's perhaps because this need to realign recurs so regularly in Italian political life (more than fifty governments have held power here since 1945) that the country people so easily accepted the runaway British officers as friends, insiders, almost family, though a few weeks before they were, at least officially, enemies.

The drumbeats and shouts begin to recede at about two in the morning and an hour later I hear a long, loud 'Shush!' in response to the yells of some drunken kids. It is followed by a quiet female voice remonstrating with the revellers, whose voices fade away as they wander off. I close my shutters and drift off to sleep.

In the morning the town centre is empty and silent, yielding only the odd fugitive tourist like me and, inevitably, a young Italian couple clasping, kissing and groping one more time before the bus to the train station arrives, its diesel rattle wrenching them reluctantly apart.

At the station I see that a train is due to leave for Chiusi in ten minutes' time.

As Dad, Tom and David approached the southern edge of the Chianti mountains, not far from Siena, they decided to risk a bit more hitch-hiking.

Having noticed that most Italian lorries passed early in the morning, we set off before dawn to find an ambush site near the road. But it was not until several hours later, when we had given up the idea of a lift and started walking, that a small Italian van drove up behind us. The driver was amenable, but protested that he had no room. We proceeded to demonstrate our well-tried capacity for squeezing three bodies where there was barely space for one, and told him, cheerfully, to drive on. He asked where we wanted to go. Tom told him we were making for Chiusi and we were anxious to regain the main Rome road. This did not meet with his approval. Although it lay in his direction, we took a long time to convince him that he would not do better to drive away from the Rome road, up into the mountains, and that the 'Adriatico', though doubtless safer, was not our destination.

For an uncomfortable ninety minutes we had to choose between the stink of fish, or the clouds of dust which enveloped us if we raised the canvas covering at the back.

The driver put us down at a lonely crossroads. We discovered, with the help of our map and enquiries from passing contadini, that he had compromised between our expressed desire and his own concern for our safety. He had given us a good lift but had deposited us a considerable distance from the main road. From a nearby hill we could see, to our west, the blue waters of Lake Trasimeno, sparkling in the sun. We stopped at the next farmhouse, where they gave us a liberal allowance of bread, ham, cheese and wine, and asked to take it away with us – an arrangement which suited us admirably, for we generally had to eat lunch surrounded by a bevy of curious people, come to ask questions and 'see the animals fed'.

A long, cross-country ramble to get back to the main road. The sky was clear and the sun scorching. In every vineyard women in brightly coloured blouses were picking the ripe grapes into large round bins, to be loaded later onto carts drawn by slowly plodding oxen. Sore feet somewhat detracted from my enjoyment of the scene – it would have been nice to bathe in Lake Trasimeno. After a long climb, we found ourselves within a hundred yards of the road:

83

enquiries revealed that we were only nine miles from Chiusi.
Thanks to this morning's lift we had covered the equivalent
of three or four days' walking.

The van driver was only one of several people who
advised the escapers to keep well away from the main roads.

For the last two or three days every Italian had warned us to
beware of Tedeschi *and begged us to stick to the woods and*
mountains. We had become so inured to (and even irritated
by) this advice, which we dismissed as 'just Italian wind',
that we narrowly avoided walking right into a small
German encampment.

To the left lay the town, immediately below us the rail-
way, and to our right this encampment. In front of us
stretched a flat and open plain of marshy meadows and
ploughed fields. On the other side, about a mile away, rose a
steep and wooded hillside with a few scattered houses. To be
less conspicuous, we separated, crossed the railway at
different points, and started walking across the open valley,
casting an occasional uneasy glance over our shoulder to
make sure we were not being followed.

It was getting dark as we reached the other side and began
to climb. We tried each house in turn but with no success:
they had all seen us coming across the plain and were afraid
lest the Germans might also have observed us. We were dead
beat and things were looking bad.

Through the trees, right on top of the hill, we could
discern the gabled roofs of a large red building. Despite our
disappointing experiences of big houses, we had no other
choice. We fought our way through the thick undergrowth
towards it.

The house turned out to be in the process of construction. Satisfied that no one was about, we picked our way in between piles of planks, scaffolding and buckets of white-wash. Since only about half an hour's light remained, we decided to spend the night here.

We had one tin of Red Cross food left – a steak-and-kidney pudding. David appointed himself chef and started to collect wood for a fire . . .

This was the night of 30 September–1 October 1943. By hitch-hiking whenever possible the escapers were managing to stick to their planned schedule. In about a fortnight they had covered more than half the distance to Rome.

My little country train trundles quietly through the *Crete Sinese*, then makes a loop round the town of Asciano. The views from the railway line are not always the best, but it is still a soothing, old-fashioned feeling to be rolling gently from one village to the next, stopping to exhale and inhale just two or three passengers at a time. In an hour or so I reach my destination, Chiusi.

The railway station is outside and below the city, and there is a hotel just around the corner. I have reasons for wanting to stay near Chiusi station – an involuntary haunt of the escapers somewhat later in their adventures. I set my bag down in a clean and comfortable room and take out my map.

Whichever way I look at it, I can't figure out where the escapers crossed the plain in view of the German camp. It's just impossible to align the town, the railway, the hills opposite and the flat plain below. The nearest 'match' would have the escapers facing north, circling round

Chiusi to the northwest, which seems very unlikely. More likely Dad's memory slipped up for once. He kept detailed diaries for the first months on the run and managed to retain them, by concealing them in the lining of his jacket sleeve, through several captures. But they were eventually found and confiscated, and he never saw them again. He always maintained that the act of writing events down in the first place greatly helped him commit them to memory, making it easy to recall them in vivid detail later. He wrote the final draft of his book in 1946, while still recovering from his wartime experiences. It covers the period from September 1943 to April 1945. Though he and other writers stress that when you're on the run your memory is incredibly sharp, it would be extraordinary if every detail were precisely accurate. I have already seen in the Chianti mountains that there are passages which, when put under the microscope, become decidedly hazy. This seems to be the case outside Chiusi too.

At first this failure to find the spot frustrates me, but suppose I did manage to pinpoint it ... So what then? I would make my way out there, discover that the land has been drained and a housing estate built where the German camp was; I might even light upon the big house, unfinished in 1943, but I really wouldn't ferret out anything more about them. No-one talked to them then, no-one offered to put them up, no-one would remember three of the hundreds, maybe thousands, of suspicious-looking strangers wandering around the country at that time. It all seems pretty hopeless. There was that one moment, when I discovered that Giuseppe's uncle had mended the escapers' shoes, when I seemed to be connecting, but old Aldo the cobbler is long dead, and probably wouldn't have remembered anything except their shoe sizes if he were still alive.

Have I really left it too late? Must the passage of time have erased the ghosts of the escapers? Have individual experiences and feelings now dissolved into mere objectified 'history'? Maybe I should simply call it a day and go back to England.

Not yet, I tell myself: sooner or later someone, somewhere, will recall something. I shall just have to press on, as they did, trusting that my luck will change, as theirs did.

After another couple of days' failed hitching around Chiusi, something odd and unexpected happened. David quite suddenly announced that he had found a bike in a shed nearby. He was going to try to get hold of it, by hook or by crook. If he succeeded he'd go on alone. There's no inkling in Dad's book why David decided to do this, no indication of friction between the three of them, or dis-agreement over routing or means of travel. For their parts, Dad and Tom had no intention of splitting up. Tom was on the run alone briefly in north Africa after his first capture and said it was the most frightening, dispiriting experience he had ever had.

We said goodbye affectionately, but casually.

'Well, so long, old boy. Mind you don't end up in jug. If you don't turn up by this evening we'll know you've got one [a bike].'

'Arrivederci! *And best of luck.'*

They never saw David again during the war, though he survived it and met up with Dad again after reading the first edition of his book. That evening Dad noted that it felt odd sleeping only two under their single blanket.

The next morning he and Tom set off southwards, round the outskirts of Chiusi.

A two hours' march, with occasional leaps off the road into the ditch, to conceal ourselves from German lorries, brought us to the outskirts of Città della Pieve. A comparatively short detour was necessary to avoid the town. Regaining the road, we noticed a small black van drawn up in front of some cottages. We considered asking the driver for a lift, but the van's number plate looked un-Italian, so we decided not to risk it and made our way round the back of the cottages.

About a mile further on, we came upon what appeared to be an ideal ambush site. The road ran along an embankment. From the bottom, although ourselves concealed, we could keep under observation a short curve of the road about 300 yards back. There were several trees in between, but one could see enough to distinguish a German from an Italian lorry.

Tom spread out lunch: macaroni, bread, Red Cross cheese and chocolate. The cold macaroni looked a revolting, glutinous mess – the tomato juice had seeped through the paper, turning it a dirty orange – but it didn't taste bad.

While we were eating, the small black van appeared round the corner and drove by.

'I think it was a Jerry,' I remarked.

'Lucky we didn't ask it for a lift.'

We spread open our maps and went over the route we

*intended to follow for the next few days. We had decided to
make for a little place called Santa Lucia, east of Rome,
which we hoped to reach within three weeks.*

*'That means averaging about twelve miles a day. Should
be O.K., even with bad feet.'*

*'And surely,' I exclaimed, 'our chaps will have advanced a
good way to meet us by that time.'*

*The events of the next few seconds were so utterly
unexpected that we had no time even to feel afraid. A
tornado down the bank, the flash of field grey uniforms, the
glint of black steel. A hoarse shout:*

'Hände hoch, Hände hoch!'

*'Oh, we've had it now,' Tom said as we raised our hands
above our heads.*

*These were two Nazis. One a strapping fellow, crouched a
few yards in front, covering us with his Luger, whilst the
other ran over our pockets.*

'Englander?' he demanded.

Tom and I looked at each other. 'Ja,' I answered.

*There was no point in trying to bluff our way out. Our
tell-tale possessions were strewn on the ground in front of
them: the map, English Red Cross stuff, slabs of chocolate
labelled 'Cadbury'. The full extent of the disaster had not yet
impinged on my mind.*

I get up early on my first morning in Chiusi, planning
to make a day trip to Città to find the capture site. The
temperature has dropped suddenly overnight and the air
is nippy and foggy. On strolling down to the bus stops outside the train station, I find that all the morning buses
have already gone. The Italian day starts early, around
dawn, and all the morning buses to Città run between

6.15 and 7.30. It is now 8.00, and there isn't another until two in the afternoon.

So I think I'll walk. The thought comes rapidly, easily. Dad reports that this leg of his journey takes only about two hours, but that isn't really the point. Quite suddenly I am back into the rhythm, the pace of walking, a state I haven't been in since the mid-1970s, when I walked or paddled everywhere I wanted to go in Amazonia. I've almost forgotten that leg power, sustained over time, really does get you places. In this sense, if this alone, I am back in tune with the escapers, as they too consulted their map and worked out their daily mileage rate, only moments before they were nabbed.

At the hotel my landlady chuckles at the prospect of my walking to Città, but tells me I should take the underpass by the station, then carry straight on. It will lead to the right road. I cast around a bit in the mist before guessing that I slightly misunderstood her. She must have meant I should take the underpass in the station proper, which connects all the platforms to the entrance. After marching boldly to the end, then up, I stroll across a couple of empty lines to a series of company buildings marked 'Access Forbidden'. At that moment a station worker rounds the corner in front of me and asks politely what I am doing. I tell him I am on my way to Città della Pieve and have been instructed to take the underpass. He agrees, but points to a canopied entrance about three hundred metres up the track. That, he explains, is the public *sottopassaggio*. Still, as I got this far I might as well carry on through the railway yard, then out onto the road. So I wander on through disused sidings and engine sheds, all shrouded in mist.

The dingy scruffiness of the station's backstage is wonderfully evocative and I feel that I can almost see the German guardhouse, the Allied bombers roaring overhead (my landlady told me the station was bombed several times during the war). The sudden chill in the misty air this morning reminds me of Dad's and Tom's decision to press south before winter set in, while the bleak greyness of the place seems almost a reflection of the numbing misery that must have enveloped them after their capture.

It's a lovely walk, packless, though steadily uphill all the way to Città della Pieve. A fine hilltop town made mostly of red brick, it stands out brilliantly against the dazzling Tuscan sky. Nowadays the main road runs round the base of the town walls, leaving the centre free from heavy traffic. Following it, I spot a dirt track running below and more or less parallel to the main road. It is well shaded, with plenty of cover, almost certainly the route Dad and Tom took to avoid the town. Staying on the main road myself, I continue along the side of the hill until I come to a rather ramshackle huddle of cottages. These are the buildings Dad and Tom skirted round after they spotted the black van.

I follow the road out of Città, looking back over my shoulder many times, checking the lie of the land. I soon find the only spot matching Dad's details. Some bushes and trees provide a thin screen at the bottom of the bank below the road. This must be where they were taken. That tingling sensation on the back of my neck returns as I sit watching a couple of lorries come round the bend and along the embankment. I can see their Italian number plates quite easily.

It's not hard to conjure up the scene. I cross to the other

side of the road, then sneak up on the ditch, as the two Germans must have done. I wonder if Dad went deadly pale, feeling the cold sweat run down his back, the way I had seen him after his nightmares and at the moment he heard of his mother's death. I bet he did.

CHAPTER SEVEN

'Rudolf is no end pleased with himself.'

'He'll probably get promoted for this, the bastard,' said Tom, with a puckish grin at our captors.

Then we got the first clue to the mystery of our recapture. Parked up a side turning stood the small black van which we had observed stationary outside the cottages. They must have driven a few hundred yards past, and crept back on foot to pounce upon us from above. Perhaps they had first spotted us from inside one of the cottages as we were snooping round the back gardens, and afterwards set out to look for us. I cursed our lack of discretion, and negligence: we had under-estimated the enemy.

'Rudolf' opened the door at the back, roughly motioned us inside, and locked us in.

'Get hold of the diaries,' whispered Tom. 'They put them back in the haversack – down there, by your knee.'

I rescued mine and concealed them in the torn lining, up the right sleeve of my old jacket.

Soon we were entering the town of Città della Pieve. The

*van drew up before a large stone building; a heavy iron gate
swung back slowly on its hinges, and we entered the courtyard of the German Headquarters. Rudolf threw open the
back of the van and we got out. A few German soldiers and
uniformed* carabinieri *were lounging about the courtyard.
Idly curious, they looked us over. Rudolf, looking self-
important, was consulting with the under-officer; the other
Nazi produced a camera and asked if he could take our
photographs. A German sauntered up and addressed us in
American: Were we hungry? We said yes on principle. Rudolf
pointed me out to the others and made some remark about me.
I asked the one who spoke American what he had said.*

*'He says, with your height and blue eyes you look like a
German.'*

I was not flattered.

*The under-officer, accompanied by Rudolf and two
Italian* carabinieri, *indicated that we were to leave. The big
gate swung open. One of the carabs led the way, across the
Piazza, with the remainder of our escort following behind.
Italians stopped and stared at the little procession; some girls
giggled inanely.*

'Looks like the civil clink,' said Tom.

It was: a large, grey, unfriendly building.

I retrace my steps to Città, arriving in the central piazza
just before the Tourist Information Office closes for
lunch. Before I can say anything, the lady behind the
counter produces a town map and marks up all the
churches, palaces and other monuments that are open to
the public today. She is somewhat taken aback, however,
when I ask her where the *carabinieri* and *Tedeschi* headquarters were during the war.

As she doesn't know their whereabouts, I get her to mark the current *carabinieri* offices on my town map. There I am informed that in the war the *carabinieri* HQ was in the centre of town, in the Piazza Gramsci.

Città della Pieve is a very small place – five minutes' walk from one end to the other – so I return to the cathedral square. Piazza Gramsci is bounded on one side by the enormous walls of the cathedral and, opposite, where the police station had apparently been, there is an unimposing stone and brick building, currently offices on the ground floor, apartments above. According to Dad, German HQ is across the square in a grey stone building.

The only one that fits the bill is faced in part with grey stone – the Palazzo della Corgna, a fine Renaissance mansion, now used as an extension to the University of Perugia. I walk in, through enormous doors, to an open courtyard surrounded by high windows. The front gate could be swung open, admitting a small black van to the courtyard. With the gates closed it is a dismal, lifeless place, its grey stone and barred ground-floor windows lending a decidedly gaol-like character. I decide to try to get confirmation that it had been the German HQ, but no one replies to my loud knocks.

Over lunch an elderly priest confirms that the Germans had indeed used the Palazzo della Corgna as their HQ. I return to the Palazzo. There is still no one there. And still I feel no contact with the escapers, even as I wander round the very places where they were held captive. This is really becoming hopeless.

I spend the early part of the afternoon looking at pictures by the great Perugino, Città's most famous son, and wandering through the dark medieval streets, one of them colourfully named Kiss-the-Ladies Alley. Beyond it, on the edge of town, there is a small tree-lined square which is also the bus terminal. Benches are scattered under the trees and on this fine, warm day several of them are occupied by elderly men. I find from the timetable that I've just missed a bus. There isn't another for an hour. A few feet away a man of about seventy looks up at me with a slightly quizzical expression. I ask him politely if by any chance he was here during the war. His face immediately lights up.

Yes, he was only a boy at the time, but he remembers it well. I ask him where the German HQ had been. He confirms that it was in the Palazzo della Corgna and, with a little gesture, he adds, 'Please allow me to accompany you there, *signore*.'

He tells me he was about fourteen when the Germans took over and requisitioned the Palazzo. I ask him what they were like and unhesitatingly he replies that some were good, some bad, just like any other people. They hadn't particularly mistreated the townspeople, though they had shot some farmers, for harbouring prisoners. He shows me where he was born, in the centre of town, right next to where the great *Il Perugino* had been born getting on for five centuries earlier. We go first to the *carabinieri* HQ, where he points to little slits in the stonework at first-floor level: 'Rifle slits, those; the *carabinieri* fired down those slits when the Partisans came into town after the war, warning them to leave the officers alone.'

We walk back up to the German HQ, the same steps Dad and Tom took from the police cells for interrogation. Dad's words echo in my mind as we too cross the square.

We were led away by the jailer, a friendly little man in civilian clothes, who did his best to cheer us up by promising us food shortly. The cell in which we were locked was minute and already almost filled with a large wooden table. We dumped our kit on the floor and seated ourselves, side by side, on the table.

Only then did the full realisation of our fate strike home to us. What utter fools we had been, and what a glorious opportunity chucked away! Why on earth hadn't we stuck to the mountains, as every Italian had told us? Oh, Santa Lucia!

'If ever I get away again,' said Tom, 'I shall go straight to the highest mountain I can find and stay there until our troops come.'

And how happy we had been! One never realises the extent of one's fortune until it is torn away. A beam of sunlight percolated through the tiny window at the top of our cell. Outside, the whole country would be basking in it: outside, bunches of grapes hung in clusters from the kitchen ceilings of contadini *houses: everywhere, friendly people were waiting to welcome thirsty travellers with a litre of good, red wine. Outside . . .*

Standing in the courtyard of German HQ, my guide explains that the German offices were on the ground floor, while interrogations took place on the first floor. The Germans occupied the town in the middle of September 1943 and the Allies finally drove them out on 19 July 1944, nine months later. Then quite suddenly he remembers the prisoners he saw here – young men, parachutists: they were all parachutists, he recalls. There were fourteen of them – English, Americans, New Zealanders.

The Germans brought them right here, to where we are standing, to await interrogation. He watched them being marched in.

At first I don't quite follow what he is saying. Was there some sort of airborne assault in the final Allied attack on the town? No, no, they were escaping from a plane. It was a *Fortaleza Volante*, a 'Flying Fortress', a huge American bomber. It was hit on a raid up north and it came down in the woods north of the city. The pilot, co-pilot and three other crew members stayed aboard and were all killed, but the other fourteen crew had jumped, landed, and then they were captured and brought in here, like Dad and Tom. I ask him when this happened and he replies confidently that it was very early in October 1943. This is exactly the time Dad and Tom were taken – 3 October. He says he also saw several other prisoners brought in to the Germans at that time, some dressed as civilians, though he can't remember anything specific about them. I ask him if by any chance one of them was very tall and wearing pink trousers. He can't remember.

So perhaps the Germans in the black van were not just on a routine patrol; they may well have been out looking for downed Allied fliers on the run. Perhaps Dad and Tom were more unlucky, less clumsy, than they thought.

The old man remembers that a relative of his was brought in from the countryside because he had lived in Chicago for several years before the war. He was made to act as interpreter with the prisoners. It was all very exciting for a young lad.

As we return to the bus stop, the old man turns and stares back at the tall tower in the middle of town. 'There was a German sniper up there at the end,' he tells me. 'He held off the British boys for nearly two days. They couldn't move forward. He shot lots of them. In the end they brought up a marksman with a telescopic sight. When he fell he came crashing down, all the way into the street. I remember seeing his body lying there, covered in blood. We took him away and buried him when the Allies moved on.'

As we pass a huge fortress opposite the police station, my guide gives me a parting shot. Inside there, he explains, in 1504 Cesare Borgia gave orders that two local princes, Orsini and Gravina, whom he suspected of treachery, be strangled in the presence of his protégé, Machiavelli. Then he had the entire city put to the sword.

'The Borgias gave the citizens a far worse time than the Germans, you see,' he concludes with a flourish.

On the bus back to Chiusi I realize that, almost by chance, things have at last moved forward. There in Città not only did I locate the actual spots where several critical events in the escapers' adventures took place, I also stumbled upon a local man who had seen Allied prisoners, perhaps even Dad and Tom themselves, with his own eyes.

But the most important upturn for the day is something I could never get from Dad's book: perspective. Almost the first thing I asked the old man was what he had thought of the Germans as people. His answer was simple and frank: some good, some bad, just like any other people. This is not the answer I expected, being my father's son. Dad, recalling his first conversation with the *carabinieri* in the civilian gaol in Città, opens with:

'Germans no good,' I remarked from force of habit. They smiled back uncertainly, sympathetic, but afraid the Germans might hear us talking. Presently the Jerries emerged with the Maresciallo, *a grey-haired old man, with an anxious, kindly face. They issued final instructions and departed: the carabs relaxed ...*

Dad cast all Germans as his enemies and clearly wanted all Italians, even his gaolers, to be his friends. Expecting to elicit a blanket condemnation from the old man I encounter sixty years later was my mistake. Instead, he makes it absolutely clear that though the Germans may have been the escapers' enemies, they were not necessarily the enemies of all Italians. The simple act of taking away and burying the dead German sniper has the same ring of neutrality to it. His tale of the Borgias and Machiavelli brings a deeper historical perspective into play. It is as if the German occupation was merely the most recent eruption in a relentlessly turbulent history, a history that long ago taught these people the value of detachment from other people's conflicts.

After a night in the cells in Città della Pieve, Tom and Dad are moved by the Germans to Chiusi by car.

We drove past the farm where we had spent, so happily, the last two days and nights; past the half-built house on the hill, over the open plain across which we had trudged on Friday evening into Chiusi. After a brief examination at another German HQ, where they took our money, but restored our other possessions (including the map which Tom had secreted at the bottom of his haversack), we were marched off to the railway station. Chiusi was a big rail junction. It looked as if we were going to be shoved straight on to a train to Germany.

The escapers were not deported from Chiusi station as they feared, but moved to the *carabinieri* gaol. Two days later the Germans marched them back down to the station. They were given beds in the guardhouse there, but neither of them could sleep. In the morning they were shoved into a car, which headed south towards Orvieto at breakneck speed. Dad was a fast driver himself, so he wasn't afraid, but he rather hoped the driver would lose control and crash, giving them a chance to make a break. Either way, Dad and Tom whispered to each other that they were delighted Jerry was giving them such a long lift south, towards the Allied lines. There was no crash but after a while the car broke down, so their gaoler flagged down the next passing German vehicle, a motorcycle. He curtly ordered the rider to hand over his machine, leaving the bemused soldier in the road with the broken car. He put Tom behind him on the pillion seat and Dad in the sidecar, then roared off towards Orvieto. It was 6 October 1943.

CHAPTER EIGHT

THE MOTORCYCLE DREW UP AT A GERMAN COMMAND post some way north of Orvieto, where Dad and Tom were informed that they were being sent to German Battalion HQ. There the commanding officer would decide their fate. By now they were both convinced that, with their guard reduced to a single motorcyclist, the chances of escape were real. They were desperate to make it happen, as they were sure that the German CO would send them to Germany.

I thought of those stinking cells in the jail at Chiusi and what lay in store for us; more jails, a crowded prisoner-of-war train, a long, hideous journey ending in another prison camp in Germany. We had to escape. Tom leaned over and spoke into my ear:

'I've got his holster undone.'

Round a bend in the road, a German lorry appeared.

'That's the trouble,' I shouted back. 'It might be better to jump for it as he goes round a corner.'

I had managed to work my legs over the edge of the side-car. Now I was awaiting my opportunity, a bend so that he had to slow down, and a steep wooded drop on the right of the road. Our driver was not dangerous, but he drove at a fair speed, and as he got halfway round a corner he would accelerate. A leap would have to be perfectly timed. What we needed was a steep, uphill stretch, to slow him down, and then a sharp corner. Every bend seemed to come on a down gradient. Meanwhile the kilometre stones flashed by: 17, 15, 12, 7. We must try it soon or never.

How about this? Uphill, a sharp bend and a wooded ravine on the near side. As we approached the corner, I saw, out of the corner of my eye, that Tom was preparing to slip off the pillion. The bike slowed. I seized the edge of the side-car with my left hand and tried to lever myself up and over the side. As I felt the weight on my arm, I realised I hadn't the strength to hoist myself out and collapsed back into my seat. Tom smiled in sympathetic understanding. The German had noticed nothing.

A few minutes later we were entering the outskirts of Orvieto. Well, we had had our chance and missed it. Perhaps we should have tried risking an assault on the German.

Soon the bike was nosing its way through the narrow main street, crowded with Italian and German soldiers. At any moment we expected to draw up at the German HQ. But we passed on, through the centre of town, still following the main road. I shouted across to Tom:

'Perhaps we are going to Rome.'

'Suits me.'

Before I board the train to Orvieto I take the subway under the railway tracks, then nose my way back into the goods yard at Chiusi station. The mist has come down heavily again, and abandoned rolling stock, signal gear and even a couple of engines all sport glowing coats of dew. There's the drone of a plane passing overhead and a train whistles somewhere down the line, far out of sight. I almost expect jackboots to click on the gravel and a set of field-grey uniforms to appear from behind a shed, and the sound of the plane to intensify until it becomes the roar of a Flying Fortress, scattering its deadly seed over the railway junction below.

Ten minutes out of the station I can just make out the towers and dome of Città della Pieve, perched on top of the ridge on my left. A few minutes later the motorway, the *autostrada del sole*, appears in the valley, alongside the rail track. A little over halfway through the journey I can see the road quite clearly: perched on stilts, it sits close to the eastern side of the valley. It is here that the dam burst in 1964, sweeping the motorway away. Here my life could well have come to an end, along with the lives of all my family. But then, if Tom *had* managed to grab the German motorcyclist's pistol, or Dad *had* succeeded in levering himself out of the sidecar, all that followed would also have been different and my life might never have started in the first place.

The hills Dad steered us through unfold on my left, running on until Orvieto appears on the right.

I quickly find a convenient *albergo*, at the foot of a road that appears to lead up to the old town.

The day is clear and bright, and the road, though steep, is straight and metalled at first. But after a few hundred metres the tarmac finishes and the track turns into a narrow, muddy path, rising very steeply. About halfway up I come to a bridge spanning the track and, I discover, the lines of a cable-car railway. A few minutes later a little carriage comes whizzing up the line, carrying a group of happy tourists effortlessly up the mountain. Why my landlady didn't bother to mention this way of reaching the old city I'll never know. I suppose she assumes that people who carry backpacks actually *enjoy* taking the toughest, steepest routes to their destinations.

Though it is hard work the climb is not entirely in vain, as my first objective is to recce all the older entrance gates to the city. I want to be sure I find the right one.

At the far southwest end of the city there are two gates, the Porta Maggiore, the Great Gate, and the Porta Romana, the Roman Gate. The latter, the gate I looked down on with Dad back in 1964, seems their most likely exit point, though the Great Gate is also a possibility. I decide to check it first. It is almost a hole cut in the rocks, a picturesque site, but the terrain around it doesn't tally with Dad's description. This is very precise.

Two or three hundred yards beyond the grey walls of the city, our driver pulled up and dismounted. An Italian officer in uniform, the only other person in sight, strolled over to pass the time of day. Tom and I got out too, and made a show of stretching our legs. The German produced tobacco, offered me some, which I refused, and then rolled himself a cigarette.

I glanced around me. On the other side of the road ran a low wall and beyond it a sheer drop of some thirty feet. But about twenty yards back I noticed a small path which branched off the road and dropped steeply towards some

cottages in the valley. Below lay terraced vineyards and thick
undergrowth.

The German sauntered over the pavement to some trees
and began to urinate. Tom and I, about six yards behind,
pretended to follow his example. I made a quick calculation.
Discount the Italian, who had a pistol, but was unlikely to
react quickly enough to use it (anyway Italians were lousy
shots). By the time the Jerry had woken up, drawn, and
fired, one should have covered ten or fifteen yards. Could I
hit, with a pistol at twenty yards, an unexpected moving
target? No, but then I was an indifferent pistol shot. Well,
it was now or never. I looked at Tom: he would have a
couple of yards further to cover, but could probably run
faster than I.

'Is this where we go?' my glance said.

I paused a second to make sure he understood. Then I
turned and sprinted, all out. My footsteps made a metallic
clatter on the hard roadway. The noise vibrated in my ears,
keyed up as they were for that other sound behind me. I
reached the path and dived down it. As I disappeared below
the embankment, I heard three muffled cracks, but no
whistling bullets.

Dad crashed through a gate and hurtled down a
terraced vineyard; then he hid in a brackish stream,
having covered himself with mud and brambles, and
remained there until dusk. His reasoning was that his
pursuers would not expect him to hide so close to his point
of escape. They would send out search parties further
afield to look for him. He told me this when we were in
Orvieto together in 1964.

I am standing at the first bend below the Porta

Romana. It is indeed about two hundred yards from the gate, has trees in the right position, and a sheer drop capped by a low wall edging the rim of the bend. And there is a small path running off the road just below the bend. A notice declares 'Access Forbidden'. Twenty feet below, there are a series of ramshackle sheds, an abandoned car and other bits of debris, including some fresh red grape pressings. No sign of a dog. I call out a couple of times, but there is nobody there. So I walk down and sniff around a bit. From the level of the first 'terrace' below the road, where the sheds are, there is a narrow path descending the hill. This leads straight down to a chicken run. Beyond and to the right I can see terraced vineyards and scrubby vegetation. This seems to be the right track.

But there are problems with this spot. For one, Dad implies that the path was above the walled drop; this path is below it. Secondly, once Dad cleared the road and raced down the path he swerved right and almost knocked a woman flying. This all fits fine with the site – the woman and her garden could well have been where the chicken run is now. But Dad says he then hurtles down the vineyard terraces to the bottom of the valley, where he hides in the stream. Today he couldn't have made it to the valley without crossing the road, as it snakes right across the downhill route from this path. The road, hugging the contours of the land, has probably not changed route in the last fifty years. So either this is the wrong spot or Dad hid in the stream before he hit the road again.

I walk on down to the next bend, where there is also a wall with a big drop on the bend itself, though here there are paths leading off both above and below it. I try the path above first, as it fits correctly with Dad's description. Here, just off the road, the gates to an allotment are firmly padlocked, and two dogs begin to howl as soon as I step off the road. The story is the same at the lower path off the road – everything barred up and nobody in sight. I decide to give it another try later, hoping to bump into one or other of the allotment owners.

Perhaps it doesn't matter which particular path Dad fled down, but on this occasion there is good reason for trying to find it. I sit down on the low wall and allow the rush of events to dance in front of my eyes, reliving the moments that would scar my father for life.

Aiming to deceive any search party by staying close to the scene of his escape, Dad lay covered in mud in that ditch for several hours. When he eventually emerged, he startled a local family out gathering walnuts.

The nuts, in their green cases, fell with little popping thuds. The small boys rushed excitedly hither and thither. Some fell in the ditch, within inches of my feet. One of the small boys crawled through after them and cracked one on a stone, a few feet from where I lay. I realised then that, naked and obvious though I had felt, I must in fact be well concealed.

My first reaction to this intrusion was one of annoyance, for it would soon be dark enough for me to emerge and slip away. I had not wished to become involved with Italians so near to the town. Tonight I intended to walk far into the country and next day to find a friendly farmhouse. But as I lay there, watching the homely little scene, I felt in some way soothed. Now the boy had climbed the tree and was chatting to his mother below. I caught a few phrases from their conversation . . . English prisoner . . . one escaped.

Since they showed no inclination to depart, I decided to chance it and reveal myself. They might be willing to point out the safest route to the mountains. I was a little anxious lest the children, in their excitement, might make some noise which would draw unwanted attention to us. That road was infernally close. I called softly: 'Amici! Amici!' And then: 'Attenzione! Don't make a noise.'

In spite of their obvious amazement, they made no commotion. The eldest boy came slipping down the walnut tree. They gathered quickly round, with whispered exclamations of surprise, and helped to pull me up through the brambles. My teeth were chattering with cold.

There was no need to explain who I was. The woman, as she ran a hand over my sodden garments, kept murmuring: 'What a disaster!' Turning to one of the children, she bade him run to the house and fetch a shirt and some trousers. The eldest son was stuffing my pockets with walnuts.

'Signora,' I asked. 'What happened to the other one, my friend?'

She gave a little gasp; 'Figlio mio, did you not know? He is dead – shot three times by that German soldier. He is still lying up there by the road.'

A wave of nausea swept over me. Tom dead – he couldn't be. Those three shots – they had been fired at me: had there been others later? But Tom never even tried to run away or I should have heard. The German must have shot him in cold blood at point-blank range. Yet last night we had been chained together in the same cell, and for three weeks before that we had slept under the same blankets. In so short a time we had attained a degree of friendship impossible under more normal circumstances. I could remember every inflection of his voice, each characteristic remark and gesture. For the last week we'd been humming snatches of Schubert's 'Unfinished Symphony'. I had seen men killed in battle, but never had death approached me so close. I felt numb with horror. My mind was incapable of realising the full extent of so wanton a tragedy.

Sitting on the wall at the site of the killing, it hits me hard. The unbearable thought that he was partly responsible for Tom's death must have passed through Dad's mind that evening. This is the root of the horror, the source of the nightmares to come. Over the years Dad told me the story of Tom's death several times, and each time he reached this moment, when he had to envisage the murder, his voice would waver, and rise in pitch. A lump would stick in his throat and in my own. His eyes would sometimes moisten, though he would pull himself back together by moving on to the extraordinary bravery of the woman who broke the news to him.

His first concrete act was to ask for pencil and paper. He wrote a brief account in English of Tom's death and told the family to give it to the Allies when they arrived.

She certainly was incredibly brave, the woman who helped Dad. Not only did she take him home and clean him up, she insisted on walking arm-in-arm with him out of town that evening, so that they looked like a young couple out for a stroll. She stayed with him until they reached a little country road, and there she told him to head for a hamlet called Botto, about ten kilometres away, off in the hills and far from the escape and the killing. That night Dad slept under his coat in a vineyard, alone for the first time in months.

The Germans ordered that Tom's body be left on the

roadside as a warning to others, but in the night the townspeople gathered him up and buried him somewhere in Orvieto. They did not, of course, know his name, and his grave must have been unmarked.

CHAPTER NINE

I SLEEP FITFULLY AND RISE EARLY TO FIND ALL OF Orvieto shrouded in thick mist. My plan had been to search more thoroughly around the escape site, viewing it with care from the city walls above, but that is now out of the question. So I follow the road down to the valley, searching the fields and hedgerows for signs of a stream or ditch, but draw a blank. I start to trace my way along the valley the way Dad and the brave lady walked, and come to the turning to Botto. It is now a small, metalled road winding upwards into the hills. Eventually I reach a second junction, where a sign informs me that Botto is just one kilometre away.

The last time I was here was thirty-five years ago, and then only for a few hours.

Approaching the first houses, to me the whole picture looks completely wrong. There are about ten of them, all detached, set in large part-wooded plots strung along the road. They are all fenced in and mostly shuttered up. They look like they were built since the war, maybe since my last visit in 1964. Then I see a large building with a tower-like structure on one side. This looks more promising. Dad writes that he spent the nights in Botto hidden in an attic of a tower-like building, so I think this might be it. But as I turn towards it a car pulls up and a charming young lady asks if she can help. I tell her what I'm doing and she explains that the old village is a kilometre or so further down the road.

The road falls away sharply, taking me past an elegant Palladian villa before I come to Botto proper. The most elevated building is the ancient church with the schoolhouse attached to it. Below them is a small new house, quite probably a conversion of a farm building. Then there are three large buildings, each one divided into several discrete homes.

A dog loose outside the new house on the edge of the hamlet puts on a great show of ferocity, but as I don't stop walking forward it abruptly changes its mind and trots over to me, panting and wagging its tail. Its commotion doesn't seem to rouse anyone's curiosity. There is one car parked in the hamlet, but it seems otherwise deserted. I look around. A single lamp post and overhead wiring confirm the arrival of mains electricity and telephone lines. Parts of the houses are clearly occupied, with mailboxes fixed by their front doors. All the names on them are Italian. In the larger buildings I can see that the uppermost levels – originally hay, grain and fruit stores – have not been 'modernized'. There is neither glass nor shutters in their windows.

When Dad arrived here he was alone and traumatized. He stopped first at a lonely farm outside the hamlet. The people greeted him warmly and agreed to take him into the village to meet the man whose name he was given –

Ilario. They set off cautiously, and just before they reached the hamlet a woman came loping up the road, gesticulating frantically. Apparently two Germans were scrounging food in one of the houses. They rushed Dad away and hid him until the Germans had gone. They gave him a meal then took him into the village to meet Ilario.

He was an excitable little fellow, with a bald head, large brown eyes and very mobile features. He looked generous and emotional. As we were about to leave, he drew me aside and asked if I would like to remain at Botto for a few weeks: the daytime I could spend in the woods, at night he would find me shelter. I enquired about food: that he could provide without difficulty.

On consideration, the advantages of such an offer seemed considerable. With food and lodging assured, I should be as secure here as anywhere else; and, almost equally important, I should be in touch with the news. I accepted gratefully. He was anxious that I should keep my stay secret, even from the family with whom I was to spend the night. Having promised to fetch me early next morning, he then bade me good night.

I woke, in the straw manger where I had slept, to find that Ilario had already arrived. As I began sleepily to don my shoes and jacket, he noticed that I lacked support for my trousers, and insisted on presenting me with his own belt – the first of many small acts of kindness.

When I was ready, he led me back towards Botto. We made a detour round the hamlet to a wood, thick in under-growth, on a steep hillside. Here he selected a large chestnut tree, found me a stone to sit on, and left me, to go to his work in the nearby fields. I spent the morning with my diary.

At midday he returned with bread, ham and a bottle of wine.
He apologised for the frugality of the meal: I assured him it
was excellent . . .

. . . In the evening, as it grew dark, he escorted me back
towards Botto. On the edge of the hamlet, which stood like a
little fortress overlooking the thickly wooded valley, he
paused and pointed to a tall, grey building which he said was
his stall. He gave a soft whistle, evidently a prearranged
signal, for we were joined by a red-haired man called
Francesco, a refugee from Milan, whom I had met the
previous night.

'Come, Francesco,' ordered Ilario.

He pointed to a long ladder which lay on the ground
against a wall. Together they hoisted it up to the top window
of the grey, tower-like building. Ilario signalled me to
ascend.

I wonder which of these windows Dad had climbed into
every night he was here. From the parapet on the other
side of the buildings a spectacular view unfolds over
woods, meadows and distant hills. However, that scene has
been irrevocably altered at some time between the end of
the war and now. About three kilometres away, right in
the middle of the open fields, a stone quarry has ripped
into the landscape. The roar of the crushing machines and
conveyor belts regularly shatters the peace of the little
hamlet. Looking more closely at the buildings, I begin to
suspect that the houses are now second homes used by
weekenders, who only come to the countryside when the
machines are at rest. Or perhaps they now house the workers who toil away in the clamour and dust of the quarry.
The distant roar blunts my efforts to get back with Dad.

*

Though there is little mention of it in the book, Tom's execution must have shattered Dad. He says he had become desensitized to death through witnessing it on the battlefield, but it is one thing to see troops killed in action, quite another to have the one and only person you really trust and care about deliberately executed almost in front of you.

At the time, though, the immediate situation demanded that Dad, like all good soldiers, should not give in to the shock and trauma. There is just no room to crumple up and grieve in the middle of a war zone. But the speed with which he accepted Ilario's offer to rest up is significant. Before the advent of the stone quarry, Botto must have been a seductively peaceful place in which to lie low and lick one's wounds for a while.

I remember I wrote to him, when I was just starting my two years of fieldwork in Amazonia, that I thought what I was going through – constantly on the move through a very exotic and uncertain environment – was rather like how it had been for him in the war. He wrote back saying, yes, in some ways they were similar experiences, but his had been very different in one crucial aspect: 'The constant threat of death does wonders to concentrate the mind . . .' he wrote.

In his first days in Botto, Dad just hid and rested. Ilario took him out into the woods before dawn and brought him back to his loft after dark. He obviously appreciated the tight security Ilario imposed, but as he got over the shock of Tom's death he found solitary confinement in a wood all day and a hay loft all night increasingly stifling. Ilario, always a sensitive and kind man, sought to alleviate the boredom by moving Dad to a remote farmhouse deep in the countryside – the home of Pompilio Nulli, his brother Sestilio, and their large families.

We set out at dusk the following evening, across country. For me the walk, first through woods and then across vineyards and over ploughed fields, was a pleasant change. Our progress was not fast, because whenever Ilario wanted to make a remark (which was frequently) he had to stop and prod me in the stomach with his forefinger to ensure that I understood. He was anxious, too, that we should proceed unobserved and he steered clear of human habitations. Once we had to crouch behind some bushes whilst two peasants herded away some pigs from a nearby field. Further on he pointed out a large, newly-built mansion situated on a hillside, which he said belonged to a big Fascist. Looking down at his face, which was normally so cheerful, I was surprised to see the savage expression on it now.

'I suppose most of the big landowners are Fascists, aren't they?' I asked.

'That's true. And this land they have stolen from the people.'

It was not the first time I had heard as much from the contadini.

The family lived about three miles from the village. We descended a steep valley and climbed the wooded hill the other side. At the top, the farmhouse lay before us, a biggish, grey building, sheltered on three sides by forest. Ilario asked me to wait behind a haystack whilst, with his usual conspiratorial air, he went to see if the coast was clear. He soon returned with the padrone, *a youngish man with a healthy red face and a charming smile, who introduced himself as Pompilio Nulli.*

I was made welcome by an enormous family. We sat down fifteen to supper. I counted, excluding Ilario and myself, four men, three women, two small boys, one a startlingly good-looking fair-haired youngster, wearing a little green hat which might have been chosen for him by an artist, and four little girls, the eldest about twelve, the youngest a baby in arms. Add a dog, two cats, a few pigeons, and the odd fowl. Once their initial shyness had worn off, a cheerful din prevailed: but the two small boys continued to regard me with silent wonder.

Of the men, one was obviously the padrone's *brother, for he resembled him closely, though he was quieter and more slightly built. The third, a dark, rather handsome little man with a moustache, wore a military jacket and told me that he too had 'escaped' after the Armistice. The fourth man was as striking in his way as the small boy. He was a huge, lumbering brigand of a fellow, with coarse features and a stubbly black beard. He wore an extraordinary little round, pillbox hat which made him look like some bizarre and disreputable Eastern potentate. His contributions to the conversation were limited. When a cat got onto the table or when one of the children misbehaved, he would utter a profound, 'Dio buono! Dio buono!' And if some remark amused him he would give vent to a loud, rumbling and somewhat disconcerting laugh. My gallant attempts at the language he evidently found particularly entertaining. I could not open my mouth without provoking that delighted rumble from the other end of the table, sometimes followed by a low 'Dio buono!' – as though this were a little too good to be true. Nobody paid the slightest attention to him.*

The greater freedom of movement and the sheer

energy of the household began to stir Dad out of his torpor. Pompilio, the *capo di famiglia*, was a very calm, almost taciturn man who made it clear from the start that he considered it only human to look after a lost and frightened stranger and enemy of the Fascists and Germans. He had no hidden motives, just a strong sense of the duty of hospitality, of common decency. As the farm was so isolated, Dad took breakfast and supper with the family, and at night retired to the stall he shared with the oxen on the ground floor. He spent most of the daytime hidden in a cave in the woods, writing his diaries. In the slightly more relaxed atmosphere away from the village, life became a good deal more tolerable.

Just as I am giving up the idea of finding anyone in Botto I notice two, then three, cars draw up outside the village church. They are followed shortly by a large van with a 'cherry picker' elevator arm on the back, the type used for changing streetlight bulbs. There is evidently something wrong with some of the tiles on the church roof. I stroll up to the group and am greeted by a friendly man who introduces himself as Elio Forbicioni. He explains that he is the *geometra*, the surveyor, then there is also the parish priest, the engineer and the two cherry-picker operators. They are waiting for a man to bring the keys to the church. I tell *geometra* Elio briefly why I am here and he immediately says the man I need to talk to is the man with the keys. Domenico Masnada arrives a few minutes later. About fifty years old, with thick glasses and a friendly face, he immediately knows who I am. And he knows all about Dad's hiding in the village during the war.

'I was too young to have seen your father, but Ilario

talked about him a lot. He was pleased that he could help your father, that he could do something against the Fascists and the Germans. He was so happy when your mother and father came back to see him after the war, so happy.'

'He's not still alive, I suppose?' I ask tentatively.

'He died about four years ago; yes, it was in 1996. His wife died just a few weeks ago.'

This is sad news, though Ilario would have been very old, ninety or so, if he were still alive. Dad died twelve years before his old friend, in 1984, aged sixty-nine.

Masnada confirms that all the original families from the village except himself have moved out and the houses are now occupied by newcomers. But he tells me that Ilario's sister Gloria lives in the nearby village of Canale, as does one of the four daughters of Sestilio Nulli. She grew up in the remote farmhouse where Dad stayed. He recalls that her married name is Ciucci, pronounced 'Choochy'. He also says that Ilario had a book about the times when Dad had been there, though I don't quite follow if this is a book Ilario or someone else wrote.

Masnada unlocks the church doors. Inside it is tiny, beautiful and abandoned. The pews are all stacked up in a corner and two pigeons flutter noisily around the eaves. Damp is climbing up the walls and creeping down from the roof, but at the far end, behind the altar, there are two perfect frescos. One portrays the Madonna and Child, the other a haloed female – a saint, I presume. I ask the *padre* how old they are and he casually pronounces them to be fourteenth-century, early Renaissance gems, which the church cannot now afford to maintain properly.

I know from Dad's book that there is a secret link

between the adjoining schoolhouse and the church, but the *padre* has been in this parish for only a few years and doesn't know about it. Masnada does, however, and takes me round the back of the confessional to a small door in the wall leading to the schoolhouse. The first day Dad arrived in the village he had gone through that door.

The Germans and Fascists confiscated any radios they found, so the people had locked up the village set in an upstairs classroom of the village school. It was attached to the church, an indoor passage leading from one to the other. After a widespread consultation on the porch, during which villagers joined us like conspirators, a ladder was produced. Someone climbed into an upstairs window of the church, descended, unlocked the door from the inside, and we followed him along the passage into the school. The wireless was a good one. I was lucky enough to intercept Big Ben striking nine.

'This is the B.B.C. Home and Forces Programme . . .'

The Italians leaned forward politely, understanding nothing. There was little news from Italy: the Termoli landings seemed to be proceeding according to plan, but no sensational advances. I interpreted, as best I could, to the Italians, who were full of admiration at my understanding so difficult a language.

After they listened to the news Ilario took Dad aside and offered to keep him here in the village, though they would let almost everyone in the village think that he had moved on the next day.

I can't follow Dad's footsteps into the schoolhouse as it is now a private house and the linking door is firmly locked. As the matter of the roof tiles reaches a conclusion,

Elio the surveyor, who has overheard my conversation with Masnada, offers to drive me into Canale and help me find Gloria, Ilario's sister. I gladly accept. A spirited debate follows between Elio and Masnada as to exactly which is Gloria's house. The matter resolved, we set off towards Canale, Elio insisting we take a beer together before parting company. As we stand in the local trattoria he writes out his address and telephone number and explains that, being the local surveyor, he knows just about everyone in the area, so if he can help in any way in the future I should just call him. With these kind gestures we climb back into his car and drive down to Gloria's house. The old lady is standing outside.

Elio calls to her that I am an Englishman, that my father was a friend of her brother's in the war. She just stands there, looking bewildered. Her frail hand rests limply in mine for a moment when I greet her, but she is already protesting that she knows nothing about this business, that the war was so long ago she can't remember anything about it. She looks almost frightened. A few moments later her daughter appears at the door. She too insists that her mother knows nothing about this, that Ilario was very secretive in the war, and that they don't know about the book Ilario was supposed to have had. I sense that perhaps there had been a rift between brother and sister, some ancient antagonism which has lingered. Both Gloria and her daughter seem keen to get rid of me and they hurriedly tell me where to look for Adriana Ciucci, Sestilio Nulli's daughter, who now lives close to the village square. It's disappointing, but then much water has flowed under the bridge in the last fifty-seven years.

Returning to the piazza, I find the place is totally

deserted and even the bar is closed. Glancing round, I see a stout woman of about sixty walking out from her garden with a handful of dead flowers to throw in the communal garbage bin. She stops and looks inquisitively at me. I ask her if she could point me towards the house of Adriana Ciucci.

She looks startled. 'I am Adriana,' she says, 'Adriana Nulli, not Ciucci.'

'*Sono inglese, signora*. My father was here in the war. Maybe you remember him?'

There was a pause. She looks at me quizzically. '*Mamma mia*,' she says. Her hand goes up to her face and covers her mouth. '*Mamma mia*, you are the son of Gianni, of the *capitano*. I can't believe this, it's not possible, you are Gianni's son come back to us ... *Mamma mia*,' she gasps. Then, recovering her composure, she takes me firmly by the arm and leads me to her husband, who is tending his vegetables, watching the scene with a wry smile on his face.

He takes my hand and shakes it warmly. 'A great pleasure, and what a surprise! Gianni's son, eh? I am Giuseppe. What is your name?'

'I am Osvaldo, here in Italy.'

'Well now, Osvaldo, come inside and we will have a cup of coffee. Have you had lunch? Can I offer you something to eat?' Adriana says, bustling me towards the door. Such a perfectly Italian reaction – the first thing the matriarch attends to on the prodigal's return is his belly.

Adriana, I can see straight away, has a story to tell. Their immaculate new flat is on the second floor, the kitchen fully fitted with mock antique oak units and a new hob, though there is also a little traditional wood fireplace in one corner. The conversation bubbles along, swapping news of our two families, of the quick and the dead. The four little girls Dad had known are all alive, but she is the only one who lives locally – her husband Giuseppe grew up on a *contadino* farm within sight of Botto. He didn't meet Dad in the war, but he knows all about him from the Nulli family. Adriana's sisters all live in Rome now, though she assures me they will be amazed by the news of my visit. Uncle Pompilio and her father Sestilio are long gone. More sadly, Pompilio's older son, Mario, was killed in a tractor accident just a few years ago. 'Poor man, he was still young; he was of the class of '30, you see,' she muses.

I don't quite understand what she means by 'the class of'.

'Oh, he was born in 1930, so we say he was "of the class of" that year, you see.'

Another little mystery solved. Dad wrote that people often asked him to which military class he belonged and he tried to explain that we British don't have military classes. He evidently did not understand that this referred to his year of birth, not his social rank. I hear the phrase used so often as we reminisce that I incorporate it into my vocabulary and learn to reply: 'I am of the class of '51.' So now I understand how the 'class' system works: it's a polite way of enquiring someone's age.

Anyway, poor Mario died when he was only in his sixties, but his younger brother Luigi is still alive. I ask tentatively about the farmhouse where they all grew up together, assuming that it has been snapped up by affluent weekenders by now.

'It's still exactly the same as it was when your father was here,' Adriana remarks casually. My pulse quickens. 'Just the same as in the war. Of course now there is only Mario's widow Elena and her youngest, unmarried daughter living there, but the house, the kitchen, is just as it was when I was growing up, when your father came to us.'

'I am of the class of '37,' Adriana continues. 'I was six when your father came to us. I remember it all very well. He was so thin, so frightened and thin. He was enormously tall, a beautiful man with blue eyes like the sky, but so thin. His hand was all smashed up – his right hand, wasn't it? He spent all his time writing, always writing in notebooks. We had to send out to the village school to get hold of more notebooks for him. He was so scared, but he always smiled at us kids and made jokes with us. I remember him so well. Then of course he came back after the war with your mother; they were on honeymoon, weren't they? . . . Yes, they stayed with us for several days . . . Your mother, she was a big strong blonde lady, I remember. We ate only the best food and drank the best wine when they came back to see us, and they stayed in the big bed in Uncle Pompilio's part of the house. We were all so happy he was alive.'

I enquire gently of the farm's whereabouts, how I might find it. Adriana says it is near Botto, easy to find; we can go there in my car.

'I don't have a car, Adriana. I walked out here from Orvieto like Dad did in the war, you see, in his footsteps.'

She grasps immediately what I mean and announces that we will go in their car. She slips out of the room while I continue to chat with Giuseppe, and I overhear her on the phone. 'Hello, beautiful. Let me speak to Grandma, please . . . Elena, you won't believe who is here! It's Gianni's son, the captain's son . . . Yes, isn't it amazing?

He wants to come to see the house. Is that all right? Fine, we'll see you soon.' A few minutes later she reappears, hair freshly combed, wearing a smart matching blouse and cardigan.

We drive almost all the way back to Botto, then take a dirt track off the road, through vineyards, and down into a wooded dell. A little car is parked on the verge. 'Searching for mushrooms,' says Giuseppe, with an air of absolute certainly. The other side of the dell takes us back into vineyards, and a further three hundred metres along stands a substantial but solitary farm building. A large dog greets our approach with hoarse howls of rage. Fortunately he is securely chained out of range of the gravel drive where we pull up.

At the kitchen door stands a small, grey-haired woman with a lovely smile and soft, almond-shaped blue eyes. She takes both my hands as I kiss her cheeks. Wearing working clothes and not a scrap of make-up, she smiles at me and her whole being radiates warmth and welcome. She is Elena, daughter-in-law of old Pompilio, widow of Mario. Beside her stands her youngest daughter, Luisa, a darker, younger version of her mother. A gaggle of boys come to peer at me, then return to their games with toy trucks and tractors in the gravel. Two of Elena's other daughters emerge from the kitchen and shake my hand timidly, along with a son-in-law. Elena beckons us inside with an open palm.

'This is where your father sat,' says Adriana. 'He always sat here at the head of the table. Sit down yourself.'

I sit.

'This is the wine he liked to drink. We still make it the same way,' Elena interjects, handing me a glass of white *frizzante*, fizzy wine. It is *abboccato*, slightly sweet, but very delicate, a proper Orvieto Classico as it should be. I sip and the talk rolls on. Elena didn't know Dad – she married Mario after the war – but she too remembers both my parents visiting on honeymoon, and the entire family knows all about him.

I feel dazed as I realize that I am actually sitting in his seat, sipping his wine, in a room that has evidently changed little in the last half-century. It seems incredible that this one crucial, pivotal place should have remained almost unchanged. A small black pot is boiling on the open fire, hooked to a wire suspended from the inside of the mantel. Next to it there is a wood-burning stove, and next to that a bottle-gas cooker. All three are in action, performing different tasks. Elena explains that in the war there was only the open fire for cooking and the bread oven. The wood stove was a modernization of the 1950s and the gas cooker of the 1980s.

A large dresser with glass doors is crammed full of trinkets, bits of china, old books and the like. Next to it is a huge wooden chest, with a lid which lifts up and various cupboard doors around its base that open outwards. It houses crockery, cutlery and some food, including bread. Adriana confirms that both these pieces belonged to Pompilio and were in the room when Dad was here, as was the stone kitchen sink, which is still fed with cold water only. In the centre of the room there is a circular electric strip light, set in precisely the position where the old oil lamp used to stand. On Dad's first night there, after supper Pompilio took the lamp down to show him the way to the stall where he would sleep, leaving the entire family with nothing but the light of the fire in the kitchen.

On the wall there are two photos of Pompilio, one with his wife Virginia, the other in uniform. They too hung in the same place during the war, where Dad must have seen them.

Newer additions include a large dresser housing crockery, pots and pans, dating to the early fifties. In a corner there is a telephone on a little table, and between the old dresser and the chest, opposite the hearth, there is a new radio/tape-player and a large colour TV. The walls and ceiling, including the chestnut roof beams, are all whitewashed, currently a rich creamy colour from the wood smoke. It is warm, snug and welcoming, a true family room for all seasons.

'He drank lots of milk, you know. His tummy was always very bad, very upset, so he liked to drink milk,' Adriana muses, watching me sit back in my father's place. There is no mention at all of this in his book, though for as long as I could remember Dad suffered from chronic indigestion. He had to take antacid pills after every meal and was never without them. I assumed that this was a result of his wartime deprivations, but now I wonder if the trauma of Tom's death had triggered the onset of this condition. I ask if the stable where he slept is still here, and with a cry of delight the whole family ripples out of the kitchen to show me to the oxen stall, Dad's bedroom.

The stall is on the ground floor, at the side of the house. Since the departure of the oxen in the sixties the room had been cleaned out, the floor tiled and a proper window fitted in the side wall. The window space was always there, however, as Adriana remembers clearly that Dad's plan, if there was a night raid, was to jump out of the window as the Germans came in through the door, and hare off into the woods.

Returning to the snug kitchen, I mention Dad's day-time hiding place, the cave in the woods.

'Ah, *la Grotta del Capitano!*' Adriana exclaims, the name precipitating a chorus from everyone, including Elena's daughters: '*Sì, sì, la Grotta del Capitano, la Grotta del Capitano.*' They all know it by name; it has become a local landmark. This leads to a second mass exit from the kitchen and we all, including the gang of little boys, set out down the track and into the nearest vineyard in search of the Captain's Cave. The youngest of the boys is called Giacomo, second son of Elena's only son. He is very young, maybe only fifteen months, but he is absolutely hell-bent on walking through the long wet grass on his own. One of his aunties picks him up, but he howls with indignation until he is set back down again. When he then trips and falls flat on his face in the mud he merely picks himself up, claps his hands together and sets off once again. His granny, great auntie and I all agree that Giacomo is certainly '*molto bravo*', a splendid little chap.

At the bottom of the vineyard there is a bank covered in brambles and, beyond that, a steep wooded slope. Adriana and Elena are sure that the cave is only twenty or thirty metres from the brambles, so I step carefully over them and head into the wood. Soon I come to a steep ledge with a vertical drop of about three metres in front of it. The woods are very like our own in southern Tuscany and I can easily see *cinghiali* – boar – pathways. These paths are helpful in unknown terrain as they weave their way round impassable objects like cliff faces, but since the animals are only about a metre tall, people have to be

careful not to get cut by the thorns and briars the pigs
walk under. Following their trail, I find the point where
it doubles back along the bank, below the cliff. After a
couple of minutes spent hauling myself from trunk to
trunk on the steep slope, I come to a quite shallow cave,
about two metres across, a metre and a half high and
maybe two metres deep at floor level. So this is 'The
Captain's Cave'.

*The next day was overcast. Pompilio showed me a biggish
cave where I could shelter if it rained ... The days slipped
by. I spent much of the time stripped naked in the sunshine.
Having got my diary up to date in note form, I began to
rewrite it in greater detail. Pompilio procured me another
small notebook from Orvieto ... Writing was the only thing
I had. When the diary palled, I amused myself by jotting
down any odd thing which came into my head. One morning
I recorded all the poetry I could remember ... After lunch I
asked Maria to bring some water, and her father's shaving
tackle, down to the cave. I shaved and washed myself, limb
by limb, in the little basin. It was a refreshing occupation,
and I took my time over it ...*

The cave is smaller than I had imagined and a lot of the
ceiling has fallen to the floor in the decades since Dad was
here. The floor itself is very soft and crumbly, and in the
dirt I find several porcupine quills. At the back there are
two largish holes, doubtless excavated by the *istrici*
(porcupine) after Dad's departure. I sit and look out
through the trees. Autumn is arriving and the leaves are
thinning, letting soft sunlight filter through to Dad's lair.
I have often, often, thought about this place but never for

a moment imagined that I would actually find it, be in it.

For me there was always something primordial about this cave. A man forced further and further from civilization, ending up living in a cave like our ancient ancestors, basking naked in the sun, reduced to a primal being surrounded by wilderness. Here Dad was stripped to the core, and perhaps it was here that the deep gash of Tom's death began to heal over. I sit absolutely still, sensing the calm of the place, feeling its womb-like security. A place of primordial shelter and succour. Here too Dad has now achieved a form of immortality. This little earth womb still bears his name, or at least his rank. *La Grotta del Capitano*!

Shouts from above call for confirmation that I have not disappeared into the abyss for ever, so I scramble back up the bank via the boar's trail and emerge into the vineyard. There has apparently been some trouble dissuading the *bravo* Giacomo from following me into the brambles, but subsequently a couple of sharp pricks did deter him. As we walk back up to the house Adriana explains that she used to bring Dad's lunch there, and stay with him while he ate, playing in the cave.

Long after he left, the Captain's Cave performed another useful function for the family, one it may well also have performed before Dad came. At harvest time the landlord's agent would come to the farm to collect his half-share of their grain, but, especially in bad years, the Nullis would hump several big sacks down to the Captain's Cave, cover it over and leave it until all the accounts had been reckoned. This ruse evidently saw the family through the lean years.

Back in the kitchen, the phone rings – various children

and in-laws consulting *Nonna*, granny Elena, about when to bring and fetch their children. Her four daughters and one son have seven children between them, with one more on the way. It's quite clear that though only Elena and Luisa actually live here, the entire family's life still revolves around the farmhouse.

People come and go, life bustles along, Elena continually cooking one thing or another, while her unmarried daughter Luisa takes charge of all the children and tends to them constantly, though none of them is hers. There is something utterly timeless about the bustle in this kitchen: an ease and pleasure with a way of life whose roots are centuries old, but which still flourishes to the full at the turn of the third millennium. As Dad put it in 1943, 'a cheerful din prevailed'. And it still does today.

I feel awed, delighted and above all incredibly lucky. In every other part of the country I have walked through, the signs are that this way of life is now largely extinct in Italy. To find it thriving at the very last point in my journey seems little short of miraculous.

As the afternoon wears on and the conversation calms down I sense that Adriana is feeling a little restless. So when she asks me if I would like to visit Botto with her, I agree at once. As I stand up Elena asks when I will come back. I suggest the day after tomorrow, as I have a few things I want to do in Orvieto the following day. She says that will be fine, come for the day and stay over if you want to. I leap at the chance and reply that I'd love to sleep in the *stalla* where Dad stayed. This gives rise to a peal of laughter and Elena assures me that guests do not have to stay in the cowshed now that there are so few Germans around.

A few minutes' drive takes us back to Botto and Adriana gives me a guided tour, pointing out who lived in which house, and the actual hay loft where Dad slept. We climb up together to an abandoned first-floor apartment where Ilario slept, immediately below Dad. Both she and Giuseppe know about the secret passage from the school to the church, as they had themselves lived in the schoolhouse when they were first married. As we look out from the parapet of the village I mention to Adriana that I think it's amazing she remembers Dad so well, considering she had only been six at the time.

'I was old enough, Osvaldo. I don't remember the little, trivial things from those times, but the important things, like your dad, you don't forget those in all your life, never.' She is right, of course. If, when I was six, a complete stranger had walked into my house and stayed for a month, and we'd played something like hide-and-seek for real with him every day in a cave in the woods, then I'd surely remember it too.

They insist on driving me back to Orvieto. On the way in, I ask Adriana if she knows the exact spot where Dad got away, so we drive to the road winding up to the Roman Gate. She favours the lower of the two bends and thinks Dad must have crashed through the bamboo canes at the top of the path, though this is not how he describes it in his book. She also mentions that the ditch he hid in was filled in after the war, so there is no point in my continuing to look for it. I leave them there, with hugs and kisses and a date to meet at their place in Canale in two days' time, on Friday morning.

CHAPTER TEN

AFTER WEEKS OF BLIND STUMBLING AROUND, SUDDENLY I am in the thick of it. Though it's pure joy to reconnect with the Nulli family, Tom's ultimate fate disquiets me. I want to make sure that he is not still lying in an unmarked grave somewhere in the city. Though the Germans ordered that he be left by the road, Dad had a first-hand report from another escaped prisoner that he was indeed buried in the city. But nobody knew Tom's name, though Dad left it with the *contadini* who rescued him. Dad never told me what happened to his body.

I know the British war cemetery in Orvieto is somewhere near the station and my hotel, so the next morning I decide to pay a visit. It is set on a little hill, surrounded by forest and looking out over a peaceful valley. With flowers and immaculate lawns, it is beautifully kept in the English style. The headstones, all identical except for their inscriptions, are arranged in rows below a large memorial cross.

Two men stand chatting quietly by a van outside the cemetery; one of them, a gardener, holds a can of petrol for refuelling the lawnmower waiting by the gates. At the entrance there is a shrine-like structure, with a metal door marked 'Register': Inside I find a complete list of all the dead in this cemetery and at Bolsena, about thirty kilometres away. I can see from the headstones that practically all of them were killed between the sixteenth and the twentieth of June 1944, in the Allied assault on Orvieto. One hundred and eighty lives, mostly British, lost for ever to take this small town. Thumbing through the pages, I discover Tom's name at the top of the third. My heart leaps into my mouth. The entry reads: 'Cokayne Lieutenant Thomas Probyn 172445 70 Field Regiment Royal Artillery Age 23 years 6th October 1943.' So he is here. Tears well in my eyes. It is both a shock and a relief to find him.

At that moment the young gardener appears near the gate, so I ask him if he knows where the grave of *Tenente* Cokayne is. He smiles politely and says he is sorry but he doesn't know the graves individually. Still, there are fewer than two hundred here, so it shouldn't take long to find him. We start walking up and down the rows of the dead. Each stone bears the same information as Tom's, and many have a little personal message carved at the base of the stone – 'Our Loving Son, Rest in Peace', and suchlike. We come to the end but he isn't here.

The gardener looks worried. 'Perhaps, *signore*, he is buried in Bolsena?'

'That's impossible; he was killed here in Orvieto – I know the very spot,' I retort, and tell him briefly what happened. He looks pale and sad. 'He wasn't killed in the battle, you see. It was nine months before, in October 1943.'

'I see. Well, let's look in the register again,' suggests the gardener.

We do, and this time I realize that he is indeed listed as being in the cemetery at Bolsena, not here in Orvieto. The gardener looks visibly relieved that he has not lost one of his charges, and immediately offers to accompany me to Bolsena if I wish him to.

'But I don't have a car. I walked out here.'

'Oh, that doesn't matter. I've got my van here, so we can go in that if you like. I'll just call my boss,' he says, whisking out his mobile phone. A few minutes later he confirms that his boss does indeed know the grave, that it is in a beautiful place and that he has permission to take me there at once if I wish. I thank him humbly and agree to go. As he puts the lawnmower away it begins to rain, the first rain I have seen since I set out on my journey. It seems fitting, somehow.

My host is called Rosario, a good name for a gardener. He is friendly and we are soon chatting away, the conversation focusing on warfare. Rosario was in the navy at the time of the Gulf War, and his ship was sent as a support vessel to the British forces. They spent most of their time searching for mines. But he had also been ashore, where he saw the devastation wreaked by Saddam and the Allied attack. What upset him far more, though, was an encounter with terrified, starving children. This direct consequence of war he found so abhorrent that he decided to quit the navy once his ship returned to base.

He is marred to a Canadian. They have a son aged three and he clearly can't bear to think of his own child undergoing the horrors suffered by the Kuwaiti children he saw. His family live in Bolsena – which we are now approaching – a pretty lakeside resort with a population of 3,000 in the winter, 25,000 in summer. Rosario tells me that it's a cosmopolitan little place, with much of the property bought up by Americans, Dutch, Germans and French, as well as a few *Inglesi*. The rain is still heavy, so it is hard to get much of a feel for the place, but the lake itself is enormous and, Rosario assures me, very clean. In the centre are two islands, one open to the public, the other bought up by a German, who has built his own private villa there. Though a Neapolitan by birth, Rosario evidently likes it here and takes pride in his rather sombre work.

As we arrive at the cemetery just above the lake, the rain is falling steadily, like English rain. Rosario fetches a huge green and white umbrella from the back of the van and insists on sheltering me all the way along the smooth stone path from the car park to the graves. On our right, he explains, is an enormous kiwi-fruit plantation – 1,200 hectares. He evidently approves of this, as many of his charges hailed from New Zealand. On our left a lovely view encompasses meadows and woods stretching down to the lakeshore and hills beyond. In summer, he says, the fields here are completely carpeted with bright red poppy-like flowers. Apparently photographers stand shoulder to shoulder all down the cemetery path, clicking away at this natural marvel. The aerial shots of poppy fields and white crosses at the end of Dickie Attenborough's film *Oh What a Lovely War* flicker briefly through my mind.

Rosario is apologetic about the state of the cemetery. He has just reseeded all the grass, so most of the ground is brown mud with just a light smattering of tender green shoots springing up from the ground. Trees stand sentinel among the graves and surround the site. Rosario has learned from his boss exactly where Tom's grave is, and he takes me straight there. The first in a row, it lies under fine tall trees, a good resting place. The headstone contains the same information as the register, and the insignia of the Royal Artillery – a crowned cannon surrounded by a Latin motto. At the base of the stone are inscribed two words:

PERFECT LOVE

Nothing more or less, just those words. And I suppose they say it all really, when nothing else remains of a life once lived.

Fighting back the tears is a battle I lose temporarily. I could so easily be Howard Cokayne, come to pay my respects at the grave of my dad's best friend Captain Ian Reid, the Black Watch, 6th October 1943, dead at age 28 years. The thread between death and life is so fine, so finite, so final.

Rosario touches me lightly on the arm and says if I would like to be alone for a while that is fine with him. No, I say, I never knew him, he was dead before I was born, it is just that he was such a close friend of my father's.

We leave walking close together under his green and white umbrella, stopping briefly to pick up a roof tile which should have been covering the electrical supply for the pump that lifts water from the lake, keeping the flowers and the dead moist.

When we reach the van, Rosario asks me if I am hungry. His wife has made him two *panini*, sandwiches, so we can have one each. He has already taken such trouble over me I can't accept, though I am deeply touched by this most simple of human kindnesses.

On the way back our talk turns to the martial arts. I wrote a book on the subject some years before and this gentle man, it transpires, is a karate instructor. We agree that the most difficult thing is to get students to understand that the aim of the art is to learn that fighting is a product of fear and hatred, and ultimately solves nothing.

Passing a civilian cemetery on the outskirts of Orvieto, I ask Rosario if he has anything to do with that kind. No, he says, Italian civilian cemeteries are often ridiculous. The Mafia particularly like to build themselves enormously elaborate tombs like villas, as if in recognition of the great and good people they had been. Nonsense and lies, he says. What he likes so much about the military cemeteries is that all men receive the same treatment there. A general or a major lies side by side with a private soldier, each with the same headstone. This absolute equality he sees as a fundamental truth. Death, the great leveller.

When we reach Orvieto station the rain has turned to drizzle. We shake hands warmly, exchange addresses and promise to keep in touch. I walk back to my hotel room and spend the rest of the day reading and writing, listening to the raindrops drumming on the windowpanes, feeling numb.

Old Giuseppe is waiting for me at the bus stop in Canale the following morning. He and Adriana first give me coffee and roast chestnuts they have gathered recently. Then we drive out to the farm. On the way Adriana explains that she has things to do and will not be staying, adding that she has remembered one thing that might interest me. 'When they decided to leave, your dad and the Australian, we knitted woollen sweaters for them. It was already November and getting cold. We knew they had a long way to go through the mountains, so my mother got us girls to knit and knit, so they would keep warm on their journey.' They used wool from their own sheep, washed, combed and spun at home. They gave them the jerseys the day they left. I ask her about the other person, the Australian, but she can't really recall how or when he and Dad met up – she was too young and it all happened in secret. She thinks Pompilio's son Luigi will know about that, and he is coming to supper this evening.

We exchange family greetings and promises to come and visit next year. Adriana and Giuseppe depart, leaving me with granny Elena, unmarried daughter Luisa and the posse of small boys. Little Giacomo yawns and rubs his eyes, allowing auntie Luisa to gather him in her arms and take him upstairs for a nap; but a furore ensues as his mother has failed to pack his *cuccho* – his dummy. Eventually a substitute belonging to another child is found, washed and placed in his mouth. He immediately removes it, looks it over and, deciding that it will have to do, plugs it back in. A few minutes later Luisa carries him up to his cot in the principal bedroom. Elena is bustling round the kitchen. Pots on the fire, pots on the wood stove, pots on the gas, pans to be washed, floors swept, table wiped: she never lets up for a moment.

I take off for a walk, wending my way down the hill below the *Grotta del Capitano* into an isolated valley with steep wooded sides and a big gushing spring, which supplies the water for the farmhouse. Beside it, overgrown now, is a holding tank edged with large grooved stone slabs where the women used to do the washing. The floor of the valley is laid to vines and there are no houses to be seen, but a little trail leads off through the woods towards Botto.

Under the trees the air is laden with the musk of decaying leaves, and all around there are little clumps of fungi. Some I vaguely recognize – Fly Agaric with bright red tops and white spots, puffballs and tall white Ink Caps – but there are also startling bright yellow parasols and some deep maroon ones that turn green when I break their flesh.

As I wander under the trees a reverie sets in, leaving my senses alert to the physical world but my mind free to roam through time and space. I have known this state of detachment since I was a small boy out alone in the beech woods where I grew up. Now that I am so thoroughly immersed, I'm beginning to see how it really must have been for Dad. He must have started to feel restless, itchy-footed, in all those days of enforced isolation. Because of his height, his blue eyes and his mashed-up hand, he couldn't even try to blend into the landscape and help out on the farm, as many other escaped POWs did. Nor did he want to move on solo. He remembered how Tom hated being on the run alone in Algeria.

Then one day he was sitting in these woods with Ilario, when suddenly they heard twigs cracking and talk nearby. Dad slipped off into a thicket to hide and Ilario went to investigate. A couple of minutes later Ilario reappeared with two men, both seemingly Italian. But one of them was an Australian named Claude. A lively conversation revealed that Claude was hiding in Orvieto when Dad escaped and Tom was killed. He heard about Tom's secret funeral and himself placed flowers on the grave. He'd been wondering for weeks where Dad was, hoping they might team up and travel south together, towards the Front. Dad took to Claude immediately and they agreed the plan. Ilario seemed disappointed but acknowledged that the longer the prisoners stayed around Botto the greater were their chances of getting caught, and of putting the lives of their hosts in jeopardy.

Though Dad didn't know this, Adriana confirms to me that the Germans issued two edicts in October 1943. First, anyone caught harbouring enemy personnel would be executed; and, second, they offered a large bounty for betraying the whereabouts of escaped POWs. Furthermore, Dad evidently didn't know that the two Germans he nearly ran into on his first day in Botto were not just casual scroungers. According to Adriana and Giuseppe they were permanently billeted in the big villa at the top of the village. It is to Ilario's and Pompilio's eternal credit that they never told Dad of the enormous risks they were taking. It is hardly surprising, though, that they both consented to Dad's and Claude's proposal to move on.

The trail through the woods leads eventually to the patchwork of vineyards below Botto. The tracks of a large tractor are etched in the mud as I come up the hill to the village. Three old cartwheels lean against the wall of an outhouse. In the only photo I have of Dad in Botto, standing with his arm round Ilario in 1948, you can see two ox carts quite clearly in the background. These may well be their wheels.

On my return to the farm Luisa sits me down in Dad's place at the kitchen table and asks me if, being British, I like tea at this time. I accept, and granny Elena produces beautiful fresh lemons from the store next to the kitchen. Her brother-in-law has two lemon trees in pots and they have fruited so well this year that he has given her a bag of them for the winter. We sip lemon tea. The house is quiet, with Giacomo asleep in the cot upstairs.

At about five, Elena's son Alberto (Giacomo's father) arrives with three cardboard boxes containing chicks. We take them down to a small hutch, Elena explaining that its door faces southeast, so the early-morning sun will warm the little birds.

As darkness falls, a son-in-law arrives with Elena's oldest granddaughter, Agnesi. I have been warned that she is an inquisitive young lady, keen to meet me as she has just started studying English at school. She pours me more tea as we play games of counting, the days of the week and the words for granny, sister and the like in English. She asks me about the Queen, about Buckingham Palace, and is it true that it rains all the time in England? I get Luisa and her to help me make a family tree with all the names of the brothers, sisters, spouses and descendants of Pompilio and Sestilio Nulli. They actually had two other brothers, both of whom were unmarried when Dad stayed with them. The older, Guido, had meningitis or something like it when he was seven, and, according to the family, his brain stopped growing. Elena chuckles fondly as she recalls the funny green pillbox hat he always wore, remarking that though he was strong as an ox he was always very gentle. He died before Luisa was born, but she too knows of him and his constant mutter, 'Dio buono'. So another phantom of the time comes swimming back momentarily, then lightly fades away in the flickering flames of the fire.

After dark, Agnesi's dad returns, carrying a large cloth-bound book. He explains that he was always very interested in the war and he'd seen the mysterious book that Ilario had. In fact several years ago he persuaded Ilario to let him photocopy it. He hands it to me. It is a typescript of Dad's book, *Prisoner at Large*, in its entirety, translated into Italian. I get out my English copy and check the chapter headings. They are identical, and random samples of the text prove to be accurately translated. Its preface seems to say that it was translated verbally by Renzo Gulizia, a very close friend of Dad's later in the war. It is dated 1955. Dad never mentioned anything about this, and nobody knows how Ilario got hold of a copy of it, but here it is – complete, unabridged and in Italian. I can only assume that Dad gave Ilario Renzo's address, or vice versa, as Renzo lived in Rome after the war. Whatever the case, it's good to know that the translation exists and that it made its way back to at least some of the people in the story.

By the time I finish looking at it, several of Elena's other daughters and sons-in-law have arrived and the kitchen buzzes with conversation about the war, Dad and the adventures of the day. At one moment I overhear one of the girls asking her mother if Dad was 'handsome like Osvaldo', then blushing deeply as she realizes I understand her.

'Sure he was. Such fine blue eyes, and so tall, but so very thin, the poor thing,' Elena replies, giggling.

The first night Dad visited the farm, they sat down fifteen to the table. This evening we are seventeen. I am of course placed in Dad's seat, with Pompilio's son Luigi on

Dad (second from right), c. 1938, in full dress uniform. Dad was the only one of this group to survive the war.

A soldier of the Black Watch at the Battle of Gabès Gap, 6 April 1943. This photo was taken on the day that Dad was wounded and captured.

Imperial War Museum (NA1846)

Me, Dad and brother Simon on holiday at Bognor Regis, 1953.

Dad, me, Simon and sister Joanna, 1954.

Dad and all four children, Joanna, Fiona, Simon and me, on holiday, c. 1960.

Dad with a 'perker' at our farm in Tuscany, c. 1980.

Postcard of Vivaro Romano, 1947.
Dad hid here throughout December 1943.

Marshalling yards, Chiusi station. Dad and Tom were held in
the German guard house here in October 1943,
the day before Tom was killed.

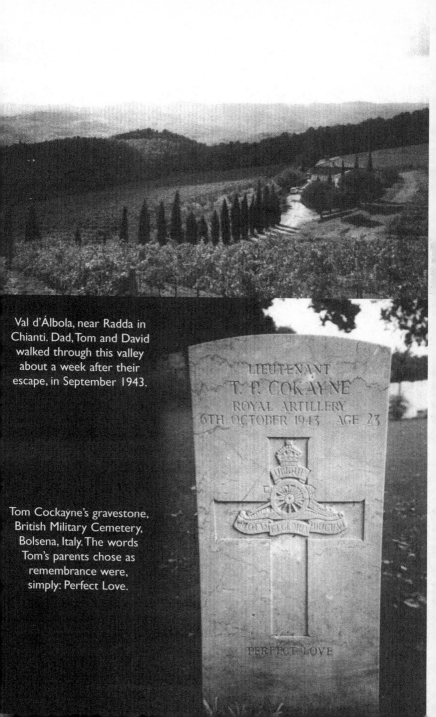

Val d'Álbola, near Radda in Chianti. Dad, Tom and David walked through this valley about a week after their escape, in September 1943.

Tom Cockayne's gravestone, British Military Cemetery, Bolsena, Italy. The words Tom's parents chose as remembrance were, simply: Perfect Love.

LIEUTENANT
T. P. COKAYNE
ROYAL ARTILLERY
6TH OCTOBER 1943   AGE 23

PERFECT LOVE

Dad and Ilario
Botto, 1947

Nicolina Lustrati on her
wedding day, c.1946

Pompilio Nulli and
wife, c.1920

Maria Cerini,
*c.*1945

Angelo and Camila
Cerini, *c.*1930

Pompilio Nulli,
*c.*1930

Nulli family,
2000

Renzo Gulizia. His own caption reads: 'I lived with visions for my country... but with assurance in friendship. Renzo Gulizia. Partisan War. Tufo near Carsoli, Italy. 1943/1944.' Probably given to Dad in 1947 by his lifelong friend.

my right, Sestilio's son Alberto on my left. Then come the other men, the in-laws. Elena's daughters sit beyond them and, on a separate table, the gaggle of children. Granny Elena takes the head of the table at the women's end and serves from there, aided by her daughters. The meal is long and sumptuous, the conversation flowing from past to present and back again, filling in the fifty years of family growth, loss and gain, regularly punctuated with invitations to come and stay with the family next summer, reciprocated with offers of trips to London and Tuscany. I have brought a bottle of malt whisky, Dad's favourite, which we men down prodigiously after dinner, the ladies politely refusing even a taste.

As the family begins to disperse and all seems to be quietening down, granny Elena explains that I will be sharing the principal bedroom with son-in-law Marcello and his six-year-old son. They will be in the big bed, where my parents slept on honeymoon in 1948, and I will use the large single bed beside it. Marcello, a really charming son-in-law, smiles warmly at Granny's instructions, completely unperturbed to be sharing a bedroom with a total stranger. But then I am already feeling perhaps not such a stranger, more a part of family legend who has suddenly materialized. At least that is how the family, how Italy, makes me feel.

At about eleven o'clock, as the girls finish washing the pans and dishes, Elena appears at the kitchen door with a large plastic tub filled with white flour, to a chorus of 'Pane, pane'. As if minding half a dozen children all day, then cooking dinner for seventeen, isn't enough, now it is baking time! Elena takes up a bowl of what I assume is warm yeast and begins to knead the liquid gently into the flour, making a little dam then adding more liquid, all the time working it rhythmically with one hand. The tub is set on two chairs close to the wood stove, which will keep the dough warm through the night. Daughter Luisa explains that Elena does this every Friday, making the week's supply of bread for all the members of her family. I watch her every movement. It is as if her hands are kneading together not just the dough but the very fabric of her family, joined, soothed, bonded by her hands.

When she has completed the kneading, Elena smooths some of the dry flour over the dough ball, draws a circle in it with her finger, then quarters the circle with a cross. Leaning low over the bread, she makes the sign of the cross many times and murmurs prayers and blessings into the unleavened bread. When she finishes she stands up, smiling broadly, and announces that she is for bed, as she will need to be up at five thirty tomorrow morning to finish the dough and warm up the bread oven. The plastic bath is carefully covered with two thick blankets, while two long wooden planks are cleaned down, ready to carry the loaves she will make in the morning to the oven in the courtyard. I watch this timeless rite in awe, my ears ringing with the childhood liturgy, '... *Give us this day our daily bread, and forgive us our trespasses, as we forgive them that trespass against us ...*'

My sleep is punctuated by little snuffles from Marcello's son in the big bed. Marcello rises well before dawn to help his brother-in-law with a chore on the farm. The little boy and I doze on for another hour or two.

The newest addition to the house is a first-floor bathroom, all done out in bright orange floral tiles. I try flushing the loo. Nothing happens. The tap in the basin is dry too, but beside it is a large bucket of clean fresh water, bracingly cold as I slosh it over my face and shoulders. Downstairs the small army of loaves are ready for baking and Elena is lighting great gnarled old vine trunks in the bread oven. Vine wood burns to just the right temperature for bread-making, she explains. Beside the oven stands a tall wooden paddle, which she will use to insert and retrieve the loaves. Two steel bars protrude from the wall – brackets for the planks bearing the loaves when they are fetched from the kitchen. Marcello's son and a couple of his cousins watch the flames in the back of the oven and try to poke twigs in, gently dissuaded by granny Elena. Mist hangs over the vineyards below the house, turning the autumn sun first red then golden as it chases away the damp of the night.

Luisa calls me from the kitchen, offering coffee, which I don't usually drink, so she gives me warm milk. 'Your father always drank lots of milk. That's what Mamma said,' she says, giggling. As I sit dunking last week's bread in my milk she is preparing two enormous pizzas: stretching and moulding the dough over the flat iron dishes, then coating the surfaces with freshly chopped tomato, onion, olive oil and lots of herbs. It smells wonderful even before it is cooked.

A few minutes later Marcello comes in, pours himself a coffee and says it's time to go. I walk over to the bread oven, where Elena is just putting the first loaves in to bake. She gives me one of her huge smiles and kisses me on both cheeks.

Taking one last look at the steaming vineyards, the chickens scratching in the yard, it isn't hard to see Dad and his chum Claude setting out in their newly knitted sweaters, into the misty unknown fifty-seven years before, well fortified by their stay with this lovely family.

CHAPTER ELEVEN

*Pompilio had gone into town with Claude's protector and
the small boy. After supper he returned with a new pair of
trousers which a family in Orvieto had given him for me. I
was glad to have them, as my pink pair were certainly past
their prime. He has also brought some strips of fine leather
with which to cover the open toes of my shoes. And Claude's
friends had sent him a much-needed pair of boots. So we
were well equipped for our journey south.*

*Bedtime arrived, Pompilio tethered his cow in another
stall, and Claude slept at the other end of my manger.*

*Next morning I led the way down to my cave in the
woods and we lit a fire. As several last-minute preparations
still remained, the family had persuaded us to stay for lunch
and to set off in the early afternoon. The new trousers were
tight in the waist and a couple of inches too short, and
Pompilio's wife said she would let them out. One of his
brothers was tacking the leather onto my shoes. Then there
was the matter of my diary, which now filled two notebooks.
We were anxious to travel as light as possible, with no*

incriminating documents. If we bumped into any Fascists we were finished, anyway: but, with Germans, we might just bluff our way through as Italians. I decided to secrete the notebooks once more, in the sleeves of my jacket. One of the women undertook to sew two new secret pockets into the lining of the sleeves. When we returned to the farm for lunch, all these preparations were completed. Between them they had done marvels. The trousers fitted, the shoes looked as good as new, and the notebooks were stowed inconspicuously away. We sat down to a huge farewell lunch and a bottle of Pompilio's best wine.

As we were finishing, his married brother came in. He had been over to a nearby farm owned by relatives. This family had offered to look after both of us, for alternate weeks, if we cared to remain a little longer. The whole family begged me to stay. I was deeply moved. Unlike Claude in Orvieto, I had been a complete liability to these kindly people. I could do no work, they already had thirteen mouths to feed, and I had no influential friends who brought me food and money. I thanked them gratefully and tried to explain once more our reasons for declining. Then I asked for pencil and paper and wrote a note for our occupying forces. Pompilio gave us an introduction to a family who lived about six miles away, where we could spend the night.

Leave-taking was a trying business. Though anxious to be on the move, I was genuinely sorry to say goodbye to this charming family. I shook hands, promised to write from England and to visit them again some day. Pompilio's brother walked with us for a few hundred yards to point out the route. When we wished each other farewell, he had to turn away to prevent himself from breaking down.

Feeling rather sentimental, we walked on, when I noticed old 'Dio Buono'. He was squatting alone on the hillside, throwing stones at a herd of swine.

'I suppose I ought to go and say goodbye to him too,' I said to Claude.

We climbed the hill to where he was seated. I told him we were leaving and held out my hand. He looked up, his big mouth fell open, and he broke into a loud chuckle. My Italian had usually been too much for him, and now this 'Australiano' was the last and richest joke. Claude and I found ourselves giggling back; soon all three of us were convulsed. We left him, still chortling with pleasure, and hurling rocks at his wretched pigs.

'Dio Buono, questi Inglesi, Dio Buono!'

The next day Dad and Claude managed to purloin a good map of central Italy from some unsuspecting villagers. They then planned their route, aiming to get high into the Sabini mountains, which run to the northeast of Rome. Leaving Rome to their right they would head southwards, expecting to meet the Allied advance. Their first task, though, was to slip down the Tiber valley, keeping off the main road and searching for a point where they could cross the river and make their way into the mountains. They eventually found a group of friendly farmers who took them over the river by moonlight in an oxcart.

As I think my chances of emulating that feat more than half a century later are slim, I decide to pick up their trail after they crossed their next major obstacle, the river Nera. A year has slipped by since my first walk, and it's now mid-October 2001. After a couple of days making grappa and sampling the new vintage with my neighbours in Tuscany, I take the train round through Rome to the little town of Narni, in southern Umbria. Dad and Claude accidentally stumbled into this same station while trying to find the bridge over the river. It was seething with Germans and they had to endure a hair-raising walk right through their midst before they found and crossed an unguarded bridge.

I set out from Narni station on a perfectly clear day, though to my prejudiced eyes the sky seems a little less dazzlingly blue here in Umbria than in Tuscany. Skirting the suburbs of the new town I soon come to a small wooden bridge. The river isn't wide, but it's deep and fast-flowing. On the other side a dirt track leads to a major road running round the base of a steep hill. Narni Alto (High Narni) perches precariously on the top. The track leading to it is so steep and narrow that I am soon drenched in sweat, my heart pounding and lungs gasping. This is not really the ideal start to a day's walk, but the little town square where I catch my breath is charming and the air is cool in the shade.

It's Sunday morning and quite a few people are already milling around in the square. A young man points me to the road south, just as a column of twenty or so motorcyclists roar into town, followed by more and more bikes, until the place is clogged with them. The machines are old and noisy choppers, mostly Harley-Davidsons, with a smattering of Moto Guzzis, but few multi-cylindered Jap machines. The riders are liberally adorned in leather, hair and bandannas. Most of the bikes have had the baffles removed from their silencers so that they roar furiously when pulling power, then choke and gargle when throttled back. Apparitions from the sixties, these members of the Heavy Metal brigade somehow, being Italian, lack the sense of threat I associate with the epithet 'Hell's Angels'.

The road south runs along the side of a high ridge, overlooking a deep water-cut valley. Narni Alto is at the head of the valley. Glancing over my shoulder, I can see a massive turreted castle dominating this side of the town. Dotted round the valley below are monasteries, forts and a castellated building that looks like a small palace. It stands all on its own on the hillside, unattended, surrounded completely by forest, with ivy and brambles creeping up its walls, like something out of *Le Morte d'Arthur*.

The ground is relatively level and there's plenty of shade from the surrounding woods. The temperature is pleasant, the air autumnal fresh, the sun warm but not threatening. I get into my stride quickly, easily.

The wooded terrain gradually gives way to a sumptuous landscape of rolling hills, farmland, meadows, olive trees and vines. I expect to see a repeat of Chiantishire here, with the traditional farms all transformed into modernized, closed weekend cottages for the good burghers of Rome. I am, after all, little more than an hour's drive from the great city. Here, though, many of the farmhouses are new and they virtually all look lived in. Dogs bark furiously from their farmyard tethers as I pass. Barns are crammed with hay and straw, chicken coops, pigeon lofts, the odd tractor, seed drill, bailing machine. The land itself is mostly divided into small plots – a grove of fifty or a hundred olive trees; enough vines to sustain a large family and their urban cousins, no more; an acre of pasture: hay and grazing for one or two beasts.

The soil looks good – a golden sandy loam, easily tilled – the meadows lushly green. I catch the distinct odour of cattle dung spread as fertilizer on vegetable patches, and the stench of pigs, along with the odd squeal. It's a pleasant surprise to pass through this rich land where the 'family farm' is still a going concern, as it was when Dad and Claude walked this road nearly six decades ago. After the brush with the Germans in the station, they too had felt elated, their sense of freedom effervescent as they struck south in the late autumn sunshine. I realize quite suddenly that I already feel close to them, almost as if I was with them, their shadow. It took weeks to feel this intimacy last year. But finding myself crossing a landscape that chimes much more closely with the countryside they crossed seems to draw me rapidly into their plot.

Then again, in the year since my first memorial walk I have been working over, sifting through, writing about their experiences and mine; I have developed an intimacy with the escapers' adventures that was not there before I set out. I have also adopted a precise routine with Dad's book. Read the sections you are walking through before you walk, again when you get there, then keep checking and rechecking for the tiny details that spark people's memories, bring things back to life. Old Dio Buono, for example, while no major player in Dad's adventures, was a real character whom every member of the Nulli family knew about, even if they were born after his death. The book, after all, is my map, my key to the physical and human landscapes Dad and first Tom, then Claude, passed through.

Calvi dell'Umbria, their and my destination, is of course

on top of a hill, but not a very steep one, and it turns out to be a charming grey-stone hill village. Dad and Claude reached it on 19 November 1943. They planned to go straight on after spending the night there, but an amusing set of events conspired to keep them there a further twenty-four hours. The episode centred round the village tailor in Calvi. Dad and Claude spent their first night at an outlying farmhouse.

As there was no room in the house, they made up a mattress for us in the woodshed. We had retired to bed when we were disturbed by frantic hammering on the window, the door having been locked on the inside. Our host had been visited by one of the leading lights of the village, who was anxious that we should dine and stay with him next night.

'Probably wants a note,' said Claude grumpily, but he was somewhat mollified when our visitor presented him with a packet of cigarettes.

I explained that we wished to depart early in the morning. During the course of the evening, I had mentioned my fondness for cognac. The stranger now intimated that he might be able to procure us a bottle by the following evening. This rather altered our attitude. I thanked him and compromised by saying that if it rained on the morrow, as it showed signs of doing, we should be pleased to accept his kind invitation. We wished each other good night.

The interview had taken place in complete darkness.

Woken by rain pattering on the woodshed window, we decided to stay. After our successful crossing of the Tiber and the Nera, we had earned a day's rest.

After a gigantic breakfast in the house next door, the girl showed me the notes left by passing British to whom they had shown hospitality. They were written in dry 'officialese' – 'This is to certify . . .' Unlike the one I had given the carabiniere *the previous day, they lacked the human touch.*

The family was in possession of a large-scale map of the district, which did not unfortunately belong to them, or they would certainly have given it to us. Even amoral down-and-outs, like Claude and myself, drew the line at stealing from such charming people. We did, however, ask if we might make a tracing of it. Claude spent most of the day on this job, whilst I listened to innumerable news bulletins, in English, French, and Italian, each more tedious than the last.

In the later afternoon we set off with Pietro, our protector, to keep our dinner engagement. Our host was the village tailor. He greeted us effusively and introduced us to his wife, a round, vivacious woman who talked a great deal. As we were sipping our wine, Claude remarked:

'You know the old boy reminds me of someone.'

I had been wrestling with the same mental problem.

'I've got it!' exclaimed Claude. 'Edward G. Robinson.'

There was no denying it, the likeness was extraordinary. The incongruity of it made us laugh.

The house was remarkable for two features: firstly, we were allotted two single beds, and, secondly, this was the only dwelling in Italy I ever came across which possessed an indoor lavatory. At any other time the handsome wireless would have engaged my attention, but I had 'had' the news.

As for the supper which Mrs Edward G. gave us, Claude and I were to look back upon it as one of our most cherished memories. We started with generous portions of ham. The next course, for guests only, consisted of two large and *succulent steaks. We were then expected to join the family in their meat course, thin slices of veal with fried potatoes. For dessert there were apples. Even in post-war Britain, that menu reads well.*

At the steak stage, a man came in carrying an object which, unless I was dreaming, was a half-bottle of real Three Star brandy. When he had departed, Edward G. gravely presented it to me in fulfilment of his pledge. I felt like embracing him in the style of a French general.

They left their host the tailor next morning:

'Don't forget to leave them a note,' Claude reminded me.

We had both wondered whether our host's munificent display of hospitality had been due, in part at least, to a desire to put himself on the right side. After all he had done for us, I was quite prepared to give him a generous written acknowledgement, even if he had recently resigned from the Grand Council of Fascism.

Our vague suspicions were entirely unjustified. He refused to accept anything at all. I protested. He remained adamant: his hospitality came 'from the heart'. He shook his head, politely but firmly. In the end I persuaded Mrs Edward G. to accept it. We thanked them as best we could and went our way, feeling rather ashamed of our cynical conjectures.

My luck is a bit less good than Dad's and Claude's, but I too am soon 'taken in'.

I see a sign to an *agriturismo* which is not far from the road, so I decide to chance it. As I approach I call to a family working outside the house, asking if it's open. The man explains that the *agriturismo* is actually the next house. Have I made a reservation, he asks, as he thinks the owners are out for the day. He adds that there is another *agriturismo* that is always open and would have a room for me. It's only another three kilometres away.

I groan. 'But I've already walked twenty-five kilometres today. Are you sure it will be open?' I ask.

'Don't worry. Go and have a look next door, and if the *signora* is not there we'll take you over to the other one. We're going that way anyway.'

He is right: there is no reply to the bell next door. So he bundles me and his intrigued small daughter into his car. I tell him briefly what I am doing.

His reaction is immediate. 'When did you say your father came through here?'

'It was in November 1943. He stayed two days at the invitation of the village tailor.'

'That's funny. My father was in north Africa then. He was a prisoner of the British. He didn't get home until 1946.'

With this sudden tingling of commonality, we exchange grins and chuckles of mutual recognition. He is about my age, a *geometra* – a mix of estate agent, surveyor and property dealer. *Geometri* make it their business to know all about the people and properties in the areas where they operate. I tell him about the tailor's brandy.

'That would have been Benedetto – a very energetic man, very well liked. He was a Communist and hated the Fascists, which is probably why he wanted to meet your Dad. He's dead, of course, and all his family have moved away. But we do see his son on TV. He's RAI TV's Vatican correspondent; travels all over the world with *Il Papà*. But he doesn't come back here any more.

'There were a lot of POWs coming through here, you know. The Germans caught sixteen of them up there in those woods in front of us. They shot them all and left them dead up there, unburied.'

As I stare glumly at the woods, he tells me of other local people executed for helping prisoners and collaborating with the Partisans. His voice is suddenly quiet and sad.

'They killed Benedetto too, you know, for helping the Partisans. One day the SS came into the village and took him, along with the village doctor and two others. They were betrayed by one of the villagers. They shot them all, over there, just outside the village.'

Bile rises in my throat. To hear that someone who helped Dad so generously had paid the ultimate price is really shocking, like a hammer blow. This was no game, no jolly ramble through picturesque rural Italy. People were callously murdered here because they helped strangers like Dad and Claude. But I could see too that people like Benedetto knew what they were risking. Appalling though it is to have a life destroyed so wantonly, I suspect that Benedetto met his death knowing that he had done all he could to help his friends – Allied POWs, Partisans, Socialists and Communists – and to foil his enemies – Fascists and Nazis. An honourable death, a man dying for what he believed in, not what his superiors ordered him to do.

A few moments later we pull up outside the *agriturismo* restaurant. A charming young waitress shows me to a table in the shade outside, fetches me a bottle of ice-cold water and says that her boss will be with me in a few moments.

He turns out to be a young man who takes me to his car, to drive down to the farmhouse he has recently converted into a boarding house. As we drive he explains that most *agriturismos* didn't really do the *agri* bit, but he does. We pass a large field with a high wire fence round it and straw bales and drainpipes scattered around.

'Rabbits,' he says. 'It's full of rabbits. They hide underground in the daytime, but this evening, when you walk up to the restaurant, you'll see it's full of them – hundreds of them in there. They are delicious, a speciality of the house.'

Next we come to a large herd of creamy cattle grazing in a field – beefsteaks for the restaurant. Then there are the pigs and chickens, all destined for the table – cured raw hams and home-made salamis as well as *pollo alla griglia* and *bistecca maiale*. And naturally he makes his own red and white wine and olive oil. He even grows his own grain, which is milled for the flour he makes his pizzas from. Italians consider home cooking of home-grown produce to be the zenith of the culinary arts, and this young man is evidently aiming at just that. Little wonder that he suggests I come up to eat quite early this evening, as the large restaurant will be full later.

As we approach the boarding house he enquires politely of my business here, so I tell him. He knows all about poor Benedetto, a great friend of his father's, and of the executed POWs.

Showing me round the tastefully refitted room and bathroom, he chuckles and says: 'You English, you really like to fight, don't you? Always in a scrap or two. Still, as far as this Bin Laden goes, I'm with you and the Americans one hundred per cent. You guys should get out there and fix him good, and we're behind you all the way.'

After he leaves I resolve that tonight I will savour this fine, enterprising young man's best steak, to honour both Dad and the man who insisted he too eat steak here, the brave tailor Benedetto of Calvi dell'Umbria.

CHAPTER TWELVE

THE NEXT FEW DAYS WERE RELATIVELY UNEVENTFUL FOR Dad and Claude as they trudged south. They made good progress, skirting their target villages – Cantalupo, Fara in Sabina and Orvinio – and sleeping in farmhouses nearby. A chance meeting provided them with a glimpse of things to come, though:

About noon, we bumped into two South Africans, ex-prisoners of war like ourselves, who had been liberated from a large other ranks' camp at Fara Sabina, a village only fifteen miles further south. Claude asked them why they had remained here, for, at the time of the Armistice, they could have walked straight through to our lines. They answered that some prisoners had lately tried, but most of them had come back.

'Come back?' exclaimed Claude. 'What do you mean?'

The explanation was vague, but somewhat disconcerting. According to those prisoners who had recently returned, the obstacles which had forced them to turn back were a main road and a railway, which lay about three days' march from here and were, I presumed, the main communication lines from Rome to Pescara. The Germans were alleged to have posted sentries every few hundred yards along the railway, whilst innumerable motor cycle patrols operated on the road.

Claude and I were sceptical. The evidence was only hearsay, and if it had emanated from Italian sources we should have dismissed it as a typical fabrication. As Claude observed, after we had left the South Africans:

'It's quite a long way from Rome to Pescara. If Jerry posts sentries every hundred yards, he's wasting one hell of a lot of manpower!'

I thought that possibly the prisoners had tried to cross the railway at a point where it entered a tunnel, and where the Germans probably would post sentries.

When I arrived at the *agriturismo* in Calvi I showered and rested for a couple of hours before dinner, then walked up at dusk to the restaurant, admiring the field thick with rabbits on the way. I also noticed that, though my feet were generally in good shape, I was getting a sharp pain on the outer edge of my left foot. It is still there in the morning; not bad, but uncomfortable. I walk up to the restaurant to pay, and ask the young *padrone* for the name of the *albergo* he knows of at my next destination, Cantalupo. He is laying concrete for the floor of a new addition to the restaurant, but he immediately downs his tools and explains that he has to go into town for a few things, so he'll drive me round to the right road out of town. I gladly accept. Yet another of those 'small kindnesses' that Dad had first noted when Ilario gave him his belt in Botto. They seemed to happen wherever they, or I, went in rural Italy. An enduring quality to be envied in any society, it's an indicator of a truly 'civilized' people.

Having been dropped at the turning for Montebuono, I thank my host warmly for his excellent hospitality and kindness, and set off at a good pace. The road, mostly level, runs south following the side of a ridge; the country is much the same as yesterday's – rolling hills, the rich odours of the farmyard, warm sun, cool air, a pleasure to walk through.

At Montebuono my road leaves the fertile lowlands and strikes into the mountains. Following a sharply cut stream bed, it winds its way through narrow valleys, wooded on the slopes, with some dramatic limestone rock faces. Rounding a bend, I come upon a perfect tiny hill village, perched precariously on a massive boulder in the centre of the valley. Its medieval walls still bind it in place, stopping it from toppling off the rock. It is called simply Rocchette, and as I pass the village church, eyed somewhat suspiciously by a gaggle of elderly ladies, I notice that it dates to the thirteenth century. In those days the citizens of Rocchette must have commanded the valley, and likely imposed customs duties on passing merchants and travellers. Dad and Claude couldn't have avoided it, though they probably just stopped for a glass of wine on their way to Cantalupo.

The stream-pass through the mountains winds on for another three kilometres before opening out into rich pastures and farmland below the village of Vacone. Here the road to Cantalupo branches southwards, to the right. I can see from the map that I am in for a climb. Altitude 250 metres at the junction, 350 metres at the top of the rise, about two kilometres in front. I stop and drink a little water before taking it on.

It isn't vicious, like some of the climbs last year, just a hard foot slog, sweat pulsing from every pore for about twenty minutes. At the top a woodman is sorting endless piles of timber, dividing them into stacks for drying, sawing and cutting to length. Despite the rise, the land is all cultivated, with vines, olives, vegetables.

It is nearly 2 p.m. and I've been walking for four hours: time for a break. I find a grassy knoll by the road, shed shoes, socks and shirt to dry in the sun, unpack my picnic and stretch out.

Half an hour later I hitch myself up and step out onto the road. From the first stride I feel stabbing pains shooting from my left foot and up my calf. They are so severe I can hardly bear to put any weight on that leg. I hobble on, telling myself I will have to overcome the pain. What else can I do, in the middle of nowhere and with ten kilometres to the next village? It half works: applying full willpower I isolate the pain and force it to recede. Half an hour later it seems almost bearable, though the kilometre stones are passing unbearably slowly. The road is kind to me – quite even with only one steep rise. At the top I stop, drink water, but stay on my feet.

An hour later I can see Cantalupo in the distance, on top of a high ridge, with a big valley separating me from it. So downhill I go, using all those braking muscles on the front of the thighs, but providing little relief for the injured left foot. I pray that the *albergo* I am heading for is at the *bivio*, the turn-off from the main road to the village. But no, after struggling a kilometre uphill I come on a young man cleaning his car. He points to the very highest point on the ridge – that is where I will find Albergo Zili. A further gruelling twenty minutes uphill take me to its door, and thank heavens it is open and – a huge bonus – they have a hot tub I can soak in to ease the pain.

Next morning the foot is worse. An angry red swelling has appeared, tender to touch, and I can't put any weight on it without acute pain. I hobble down to the village and buy some painkillers but they have no effect at all. I know from my time in Amazonia that if you start out on a day's walk with a limp, you invariably finish up much, much worse off at the end of the day. There is no way I can make the twenty-plus kilometres to Fara in Sabina today. The old couple in the *albergo* tell me I can take a bus at 9.30, which connects with another one to Fara in Sabina. I have little alternative, if I am going to stay on route.

In fact the bus takes me to a train station, and there is a train to Fara. But by now I am wary of the distances between towns and their stations. A careful look at my map confirms my suspicions. Fara station is at least eight kilometres from the town, all uphill. That prospect does not appeal at all. I have a one-day travel card, and find that the train which goes to Fara in fact terminates at Rome's Fiumicino airport. By the time it arrives I've made up my mind: I'll hire a car from Fiumicino.

Though I am desperately keen to keep to Dad's and Claude's agenda, it's plain that I can't. In any case, there are other reasons to change plans. I learned last year that the sheer act of walking, other than being some form of empathetic penance, is not intrinsically illuminating. The 'Dad was here' syndrome palls once it has been repeated a dozen times. Further, when Dad and Claude were on the move they left little or no traceable evidence of their presence. Only in Calvi, where they halted for an extra day with tailor Benedetto, was there some story to follow up, a tale – albeit tragic – to be heard. For the next several days they moved fast, often cross-country, and stayed in unidentifiable farmhouses, outside the villages they name. Quite often they didn't even follow the roads:

Our map, the information we had received from those rather gloomy South Africans and our own view of the country – all prepared us for the toughest walking we had yet to face. The high, steep, and often wooded mountain ridge which lay before us looked formidable indeed.

We were to be pleasantly disillusioned. Thanks to our map, we knew which villages to enquire for, and there was invariably a small footpath, leading either through the narrow valley or else round the side of the mountain ridges. The tracks had a double advantage. They were mostly dry and hard and, unlike the roads, there was no fear of encountering anything more dangerous than a peasant on a donkey. Occasionally we had to make a detour to avoid a village, but on the whole we made good progress.

Fifty-eight years later, I have no chance of following the maze of little footpaths, tracks and detours they took, even if I was fit to do so. So, as not much happens to the escapers in the following days, there will be little more than the landscape to absorb.

To stick to the 'spirit' of the exercise I decide to retrace my earlier route in the car, then carry on through the villages Dad and Claude passed in the following days. So I leave the motorway at Narni, the starting point of this year's walk. It takes about twenty minutes to drive the six-hour walk to Calvi and a further half-hour to cover the second day's walk. Though I can follow the route without a map, I discover curious differences between walking and driving. On foot one's senses are all vertical. It's all about gradients, up or down. Driving is a much more horizontal affair. I had little idea, while walking it, that the first day's road was so twisty that I can barely maintain 40 or 50 kph for most of the way in the car. On foot, my main interest was how pleasantly flat it was until I actually reached Calvi.

Passing Cantalupo, I soon find myself enmeshed in a web of tiny, twisting roads threading through increasingly steep, barren country. Twice I get the road wrong and have to backtrack – not something I'd want to do on foot. But then we are much more cautious and enquire much more freely of the way at five kph than at fifty.

Fara is a spectacular medieval village sitting right on top of an incredibly high and steep pinnacle. It takes a good ten minutes to drive up it – at least two hours' slog on foot. Furthermore, I soon discover that there is no accommodation in the place at all. Having got up here, I would have just had to walk all the way back down again. I silently bless my injured foot for preventing me from finding this out the hard way.

This near-disaster makes me realize that in many ways Dad and Claude were better off than I am, at least in terms of finding accommodation. By this point they were not only confident of finding a meal and a bed of sorts, they positively expected it of the people. By now they were well tuned to the nuances of the situation, asking first about local Fascists or Germans, sticking to isolated or outlying farms and only using villages like Cantalupo and Fara as reference points. Thereby, incidentally, they not only avoided hostile encounters but also circumvented the gruelling foot slogs to the peaks where these villages perch.

But I am stuck with the roads, the hilltop villages and the thin spread of *alberghi* and *agriturismi* for my supper and bed.

From Fara, Dad and Claude made their way through hilly but cultivated country to a little village called Scandriglia. Here they had to cross one of the central ridges of the Apennines, to a village called Orvinio. Nowadays the track is still unmetalled and cuts through the northern edge of the Parque Regionale dei Monti Lucretili. Just out of the village a shepherd is strolling slowly as his herd of sheep and goats graze the hillside. Two large white dogs sprawl in the middle of the dusty road and only consent to move aside when my car gets very close to them. I listen to the tinkling bells and ask the shepherd if this is the old track to Orvinio. He says they cleaned it up and straightened it out a few years ago but, yes, this is pretty much the route it has taken ever since he can remember. So at least I am in the escapers' footsteps for this part of their journey.

At first the track runs up the right side of a wide, fertile valley. As I climb, the views on my left extend to a majestic panorama of wooded hills and valleys stretching away in the haze. On my right the park is densely wooded, steep and mulchy underfoot. Eventually I reach the ridge, cross the watershed and cruise gently down towards the sleepy village of Orvinio. Shortly before I get there I come upon a flat-backed van parked at the kerb. Two men are struggling to load onto the vehicle three huge brown carcasses: the first of this season's crop of *cinghiale*, wild boar. There will be good suppers in those households tonight.

From Orvinio to Vivaro Romano is only nine kilometres today, though Dad claimed the track was longer in the war. It was here that, for once, Dad and Claude came quite badly unstuck. They had just been fed by a local on the outskirts of Orvinio, who warned them that there were Germans in the village.

The man undertook to show us the way and conducted us to a little hill overlooking the valley. We could distinguish two passes, one of which, our escort informed us, led to Vallinfreda, our 'target for tomorrow'. The country was wild and rugged. There were no houses within sight, but obviously we could not expect to spend the night in an enemy-occupied village. I noticed several flocks of sheep, herded in pens in the flat, scrubby valley below the mountains. Our guide told us that they had been 'evacuated,' by the Germans, from areas near the front. Most of the shepherds employed on this job came from Rome, but he warned me that they were sometimes escorted by a German soldier.

In the valley, through which ran a shallow river, the mud was again tiresome. By the time we reached the sheep pens it was dusk. The shepherds were making themselves draughty little bivouacs out of brushwood and a few strips of canvas. There were no signs of any Germans: indeed, I couldn't imagine a Jerry stooping to such crude accommodation. We asked the shepherds if they knew of any local farmhouses, but

they were as much strangers in these parts as we were ourselves. The only sign of habitation that we could see was a
small hut, about half a mile away.

Towards this, for want of anything more promising, we
betook ourselves, to find on arrival that it was nothing more
than another sheep pen. An old peasant was milking his
ewes. One is always learning something new: till then I had
been unaware that one could milk sheep. Clearly, one could,
for the shepherd already had a small can full of milk.

About the question of lodgings, the old man was gloomy.
Pointing vaguely towards the west, he admitted that there
was a farmhouse, but it was a long way, we should have to
cross a river, and before we got there it would be dark. What
then did he suggest? He gave that familiar Latin gesture,
signifying 'Chi lo sa?' and a general belief in the goodness of
providence.

As he appeared to be the only inhabitant within miles, we
had no intention of abandoning him, or rather of letting him
abandon us. If necessary, now that it was dark, we would
accompany him back to Orvinio, and slip out of the village
before dawn next morning. The old man, though well
disposed towards us, was opposed to the scheme.
Provided he could produce a reasonable alternative, so were
we.

The milking finished, we helped him to herd his sheep into
the little hut. Certainly no further accommodation was
available there. We had walked with him about a mile, back
towards Orvinio, when we came upon a barn. The old man
tried the door and, after some rough handling, managed to
get it open. The floor was strewn with old corn cobs. There
was no straw and the cobs would provide a somewhat
knobbly bed, but it seemed as good a shelter as we had any

right to expect. Before he left, the old shepherd gave us half a loaf of bread. It was now quite dark.

The barn was about fifty yards from the river, and I thought I would stroll down for a drink of water before turning in. Claude said that he would accompany me.

We were returning along the little track from the river when suddenly, out of the darkness in front of us, came a loud and guttural challenge. For a second we were paralysed into immobility. Then I leapt, over a low stone wall, down to the ploughed field, fortunately only a few feet below. Claude, and about half the stone wall, landed on top of me, with a noise like an avalanche. We scrambled to our feet and started to run. I was expecting bullets to whistle after us, but no shots were fired. Luckily, the night was black as pitch. My chief fear was that I should get separated from Claude. We ran a few hundred yards then hid behind some boulders. Claude laughed softly:

'He isn't in the race on a night like this.'

For a quarter of an hour we crouched there, listening intently in the darkness. Whoever it was – and we were reasonably certain it was a German – had evidently lost interest and departed. We tiptoed back towards the barn, stopping every few yards to listen. Everything was still.

We dared not remain in the barn in case the German returned with reinforcements. Only one alternative remained – to try to find that farmhouse on the other side of the stream. We collected up our coats. I couldn't find the half-loaf which the shepherd had given us. We were reluctant to strike a match, so we left it there.

If the going was bad during the daytime it was ten times worse at night. That bleak moorland must have been inter-laced with more streams than any other strip of land in Italy.

I fell into eight before we eventually reached the small river at which we were aiming. Here Claude rather cleverly found a ford and we picked our way across on stepping stones. On the other side were several small footpaths.

'Surely one of these will take us to a house,' said Claude.

They didn't. We tried them all in turn. Each led, with unerring accuracy, to the next stream and there petered out.

For what seemed like hours, we wandered about that wretched heath. Besides the streams, there were innumerable small, spindly thorn bushes, which tore at one's feet and ankles. Of habitation, human or otherwise, there was not so much as a sheep shack. We walked until we were so tired we had to sit down, at which juncture it started to rain. Soon we were shivering so violently that, to keep warm, we were forced to start on our perambulations again. What wouldn't we have given for that brandy! We had long ago abandoned any hope of finding a house.

Claude suggested we light a fire. For fuel, we had to make shift with the thorn bushes. Breaking them off was a painful business, though Claude managed to pull two of them out by the roots. He found a comparatively sheltered spot in the gully of one of the streams, and used up the last of our toilet newspaper getting the fire going. That he eventually succeeded was something of an achievement. For a few blessed moments we huddled over the small flames, until the need for more fuel drove us away. We exhausted the local supply of thorn bushes, and then crouched uneasily over the rapidly dying embers.

'Look!' exclaimed Claude suddenly. 'I believe dawn is breaking.'

Above the mountains to the east glowed a pale light. Every few minutes we fancied it was getting a little lighter.

Not until the faint, silvery beam shifted very slightly in the sky did I realise what it was: the rays of a distant searchlight.

That night seemed endless. We got up and walked again. We fell into some more streams. Claude lit another fire. The rain came down harder. At last, on one of our aimless wanderings, I spotted the white walls of some sort of building. It was, of course, separated from us by a broadish stream which we had some difficulty in fording. Our feet were already soaked, but we wished to avoid falling in up to the waist.

As we approached, came, not the dawn, but a deluge. The white building turned out to be only another sheep shelter. To us it was as welcome as a hotel – almost. Frenzied bleatings greeted our arrival. Warm, woolly bodies jostled against our thighs. Claude struck a match. A sea of petulant, white faces gaped up at us: our feet were ankle deep in mud and excrement. Two stones, in a corner of the shed, offered the only seating accommodation. We couldn't afford to be particular. I sat down, rested my elbows on my knees and my head on my hands. I retain a last memory of the rain beating violently on the roof.

I slept.

The terrain is harsh indeed. And incongruous – a wild strip of moorland just a stone's throw from Rome. Dad's Lear-like experiences on the blasted heath outside Orvinio have long haunted me, so just below the village I pull up and climb a little knoll, like Dad and Claude did. It is easy to spot the two dents in the hills on the horizon, one pass leading to Vallinfreda, the other to Vivaro Romano. The intervening high, scrubby plain still looks uninhabited, though I can make out large pastures dotted with sheep and cattle, and barns to house them. Orvinio is high up, at over 800 metres, and the land to the immediate west rises to 1,000 metres. The air is decidedly cooler than anywhere else I have been, even in mid-October, more than a month before the escapers floundered around in the pitch-black night, the mud and the rain.

The road looks new, but it more or less follows the river valley southwards across the moorland to the mountain ridge. Rounding a bend about three kilometres from Orvinio, I spot a turning off the road, festooned with an enormous ranch-like sign. It announces *Agriturismo – Pianura dei Colli*. High Plains Farm. I turn and bump along a track through green pastures, past a barn full of young beef cattle. Below it, a modern chalet-like building stands alone in the middle of a meadow. Inside, a friendly middle-aged woman welcomes me. I explain that I might be needing a room. So she shows me a large, airy bedroom, brand-new and tastefully furnished, with a well-equipped bathroom adjoining. It is the best, and the cheapest, room I have come across so far. *Casalinga* – family meals – are on offer at equally modest rates. As it's already five o'clock I decide to check in, and catch up on my diary before supper. I feel just the tiniest nagging guilt, being so comfortably installed virtually on the spot where Dad and Claude spent such a wretched night.

When I come down for supper Mario, the farmer, greets me. Bringing me a jug of his good red wine, his opening gambit is that I clearly travel a great deal – he has my passport for registration. What then brings me to this neck of the woods? I tell him about Dad's and Claude's night of torment.

'They were pretty certainly on our land when they got

lost. It was very marshy then, poorly drained in parts. Two main trails led across the plain to the two passes, but the road was not made up until the 1960s. It sounds like your father and his friend got lost between the two trails. The man they met with his sheep out here was probably my uncle Alfio. He was an old man when I was a boy. He had grazing rights further up the valley.'

I ask him politely which 'class' he belongs to. He is of the class of '41. He can't really remember the war, though of course he heard many stories of Allied prisoners passing through here, and of the Germans in the village, where his family lived at the time. The conversation turns to the present and he tells me with pride about his herd of beef cattle, raised organically. I ask Mario if there are any ruined churches in the neighbourhood, as Dad mentions passing one on his way across the plain. Certainly he knows the only ruined church in the neighbourhood, and he offers to take me out to see it, and his herd of beasts, first thing in the morning.

A thick mist shrouds the high plain when we set out in his Land-Rover. As we bump along little country lanes and the sun burns off the mist, Mario skilfully redraws the landscape for me as it was fifty years ago. Here there were vineyards, producing a low-grade wine – we are really too high for vines. They were abandoned in the 1950s and the land was left to run wild. Mario leased the land a few years ago, cleared it and turned it into pasture. We cross a narrow lane. This was once the main road to Vivaro Romano; you can tell it was important because it is a full wagon's width, not just a track for donkeys or mules. Next we are in chestnut woods, each stand claimed by a particular family in the village, though nobody bothers much these days. Beyond the woods lies more open pasture, well stocked with large creamy-brown cows, his breeding herd. 'These are the mothers of the calves you saw in the barn, a cross between Charolais and Maremmani, cattle from around your farm in Tuscany.' They look fat and content, chewing the cud and exuding great clouds of steamy breath.

Round a bend, the church looms up in front of us. It is very old; a notice declares it ninth century. Though the roof has gone, the walls and window frames stand out gauntly against the morning light. Mario is certain that this is the only ruined church for miles around, but I can't make it fit with the geography Dad describes. He and Claude came upon it the morning after their night on the heath, apparently near to the pass into Vallinfreda. But we are several miles from there. Perhaps it wasn't a church that Dad saw. Well, no matter.

On the way back to the farm we concentrate on the old track to Vallinfreda, the one the escapers set out on that evening before getting lost. Mario shows me several sections of it. It snakes along the valley floor, much closer to the river than the new, made-up road. Where it took a detour round a particularly wet patch it overlaps the modern road, and Mario has incorporated about fifty metres of it into his new drive. But for the most part it is overgrown, detectable in the undergrowth but disused, dissolving into the landscape, discernible only in the memory of people like Mario. With a twinge of remorse I realize that this has probably been the case virtually every-where I have walked. Fifty years of growth in mechanization, mobility, motorization, has altered the landscape enormously, irredeemably. It seems likely that I have taken hardly a step which actually was in Dad's and Claude's footsteps, that all this route-marching in their shadows is in fact illusory. A depressing thought. Yet the search is not actually for roads but for the contacts, human and material, that bear testimony to the escapers and their travails.

As we approach Mario's farm I notice a stone building in a clump of trees near the river. Part of its roof has caved in but it's quite visible from the new road. I ask Mario if this is the farthest old building from Orvinio. He says that it is and recalls that a neighbour used to store his crop of *granturco* in it. Not quite sure what sort of grain this is, I make a mental note to look it up when I get back to the farm. It means maize. This tallies with the description of the barn where Dad and Claude were spooked at the beginning of their night on the blasted heath. It is also in the right place. I decide to look it over on my way into Vivaro Romano.

Pulling off the metalled road onto a section of the wartime track, I park the car under a tree and walk across a meadow to the dry riverbed. I can see the barn just above me. It is, as Dad recalled, only about fifty yards from the river. As I walk up the little path I feel that familiar tingling sensation running down my spine. It seems odd that this sensation hasn't gone away, that it recurs whenever I feel sure that I am very close to the escapers. But I realize now that my reaction to it has changed. Whereas last year it tended to make me feel excited, even nervous, this year it makes me feel calm, fulfilled, as if the emotional chemistry I intuitively thought might occur is actually beginning to work.

The door to the barn holds good on an ancient bolt, but

it is so shrunken with age that I can see through its chinks to the grey straw, the stalls and the fallen roof beams and tiles. Bits of junk – an old chair, a rusty scythe, timber and fence posts – litter the floor. The roof has given way at the rear, releasing a gentle back-light across the interior, setting the hay loft in silhouette. I scramble up the slope to the back of the building and manage to prise the door of the hay loft open.

Here is a scene of gradual decay. In twenty or forty years' time the rest of the roof will be gone, ivy and brambles licking up the walls. The stout chestnut timbers will turn slowly to dust. The stone walls will remain defiantly visible for a few more decades before being swallowed by the surrounding woodland. Yet fifty-eight years ago my father planned to spend a warm, dry night here, until a phantom enemy drove him out. It seems for a moment that I am looking down not at a crumbling building, but at my memory of Dad: life gone, body decayed, but still a very visible, definable structure in my own inner landscape.

Outside, I easily find the dry-stone wall Dad and Claude leapt over, the field, long fallow now, that they sprinted across, and the cover they reached on the other side. I walk the fifty yards to the river, cross it, and head for Vivaro Romano.

CHAPTER THIRTEEN

The hillside immediately below us was obscured by project-
ing crags, but we had only descended a short distance when
we came upon a narrow mountain road, with the village of
Vallinfreda perched on a small peak to our left. We
clambered down to the road at a point just short of the
village, where we encountered a peasant.

Vallinfreda, he informed us, was occupied by a few
Austrians who 'were not bad people'. I explained our plight
and told him that it was essential for us to find somewhere to
spend the night. He made us hide in a vineyard while he
went off to find us something to eat. It started to rain again.
He returned with a large loaf, which we split in two and
waded into like wild animals. The dry bread tasted like the
most succulent cake.

'I say!' exclaimed Claude with his mouth full. 'There's
another village over there.'

Like Vallinfreda, this village was built in tiers, on the side
of the hill – a considerable architectural feat. The man told
us it was called Vivaro Romano and that it was not occupied

by the Germans. It lay only a short distance away, but the grey houses blended so closely with their rocky background that at first we had not detected them. We decided to try there for lodging.

'And if they won't take us in, we'll sit on their doorstep until they do,' said Claude.

Short of climbing the mountain again, there was no cross-country approach so we started off down the road. Vivaro was further by the road than it looked – about two miles.

As we entered the piazza we noticed a group of men gossiping outside a house. I was about to address them, when we heard the sound of a motor bike approaching from behind. We darted hastily up a side alley. I glanced over my shoulder and saw the motor cyclist ride into the piazza and dismount. He was dressed in German uniform, with a rifle slung across his back. We took refuge in a pig-sty.

A girl witnessed our sudden flight, and when the German had departed she beckoned us out. I told her of our miserable condition, tired, wet, and hungry. She led us off to her own house, where her mother, a large and kindly old woman, who reminded me of a favourite aunt, made us welcome.

She cooked us an enormous dish of pasta, which we proceeded to wolf as if that loaf of bread had never existed. Afterwards she led us up to their stall, at the top of the village, where we could sleep in a manger until supper. The straw felt like the softest of feather beds.

Some hours later the old girl returned, managed to awaken us, and led the way back to the house, where another magnificent meal awaited us – this time fried eggs and potatoes.

The family consisted of Camilla, the mother, her husband, a quiet and benevolent man called Angelo, and their two

grown-up daughters, Maria and Adelina. They had also,
Camilla told us, two sons: one was in Sicily, and the other a
prisoner of war in Egypt. The latter they heard from
regularly and he was being well treated.

A group of men are gossiping in the square as I pull up
in Vivaro. I saunter over and sit down next to a severely
crippled old gaffer with a curious and engaging smile. He
wears nothing but a pair of shorts and is deeply tanned. I
tell him that Dad was here in the war, one of the prisoners.
Yes, he recalls, there were lots of prisoners here in the war.
He of course was only a young lad at the time, so he
doesn't remember much.

'So what was he called, your dad?'

'He was called Gianni, Giovanni, Capitano Gianni; he
was very tall, much bigger than I am, with blue eyes.'

'No, I don't recall a Capitano Gianni.'

'The people who looked after him were Angelo and
Camilla.'

'Ah, well, then you need to speak to Maria. She lives
just up there. See the house with the flowers on the
balcony? That's her place. Their daughter, she's there
right now.'

Maria. The girl who spotted Dad and Claude in the
pigsty and led them to the shelter of her parents' house.
And she is at home.

In response to my knock a stout woman with dark-
brown hair and eyes appears among the flowers on the
first-floor balcony. She looks troubled, startled, as I
explain who I am. She passes her left hand over her brow,
looks at me again, then comes downstairs to let me in. By
the time she reaches the door her bewilderment has

passed and her face lights up with a radiant smile. She ushers me upstairs to her bright, airy apartment.

'He's dead, your father, isn't he?'

'Yes; he died in 1984.'

'I knew that. You see, one of the ladies in the village here, she married an escaped English prisoner, who took her back to live in England. She would bring news when she visited every year. We knew that your father had some sort of job with *The Times*.'

'He was their point-to-point correspondent.'

'Well, this lady noticed that in 1985 there was a new correspondent, so we thought he must have died. He used to write to us, you know; he wrote many times. He even sent a photo of you children when you were all small. Straight after the war he sent my father a great big package of pipe tobacco. Papa was really thrilled. He loved to smoke his pipe and it was very hard to get tobacco in those days.

'My father wrote to him about my brother, who was still in a prisoner-of-war camp in Egypt. Your father managed to get him released, I don't know how. We were all so happy when my brother walked into the village. I think it was in 1946. His wife and little son Angelo had lived with us all through the war. The poor boy didn't recognize his father at first. Of course he saw your father when he was here; he used to eat with the whole family every day. I'll phone him and tell him you have come.

'Then one day in 1947 the postman came to our house with a big package. We all wondered what on earth it could be. It was this.'

She turns to her bookcase, and from under some old magazines she hauls out a pristine copy of Dad's book, still in its yellow dust cover. I've never actually seen the dust cover before. On the flyleaf Dad has written:

> *Per I miei carissimi amici*
> *Camilla e Angelo Cerini,*
> *Che no sarete mai dimenticati*
> *dal autore di questo libro.*
> *Settembre 1947 Ian Reid*

(For my dearest friends Camilla and Angelo Cerini, you will never be forgotten by the author of this book.)

'He always said he would write a book about it all when it was over. He kept his notebooks here, and he told me that if ever the Germans raided the place I was to take his books and hide them under a stone, somewhere where they would be safe. It's always been a bit frustrating for me. I've found the passages about us, but even with the dictionary I can't really understand what he wrote. I was a teacher, but I never studied English.'

I tell her about the Italian translation I discovered last year and promise to call Elena in Botto and get her son-in-law to send a copy to Maria.

Staring rather serenely at the wonderful view through her window, she muses: 'He was such a fine man, your father, such a gentleman. My father and mother adored him. And now you have come. I'm so happy that you are here, that the good Lord has sent you to me. You will stay for lunch.'

It isn't an offer, it's just stating the obvious: all English waifs and strays must be fed. I perform the ritual 'No, no, there is no need' rather feebly. As she sets about making fresh pasta I ask her about her family. They are nearly all gone. She was twenty-two when Dad was here; her little sister sixteen. Adelina had died young, as had her brothers. Now there is only her nephew, little Angelo, who lives in Rome but comes out here for weekends. He has the apartment above hers, on the second floor. She asks after my mother and tells me about the honeymoon visit. They all went down to Dad's favourite spot, Angelo's kitchen garden, where they had a big picnic. She remembers Mum as very tall and fair, but unable to speak Italian. As she talks, I catch just the faintest whiff of passion for Dad. I ask her if she had married, but, no, she hadn't, ever, and now she's eighty it seems a bit unlikely, she adds, chuckling.

With the initial rush of news and recollections past, I judge it time to start going over the ground with some care. It's really extraordinary to be talking with someone who was a fully grown adult when Dad was here.

'It was you who first spotted Dad and Claude and brought them to your parents. Was it to this house?'

'Yes, I brought them here. This room we're in now was the kitchen. Your father used to sit over there, by the window. But it didn't happen like that. What really happened was that Mamma was looking out of the window when the German rode in on his motorbike. She saw these two men scuttling away from the German and hiding. She knew they were strangers – we know everyone in the village – and she guessed they were escaped prisoners. Then she thought of her own son, my brother, in prison in Egypt and how one day he too might be on the run. So she told me to go down and fetch those poor boys as soon as the German had gone. That's what really happened.'

Dad delivered from evil by maternal affection. It adds up.

'After that we did everything for them – washed and mended their clothes, fed them, found them safe places to sleep. They were officers, after all, and they didn't know how to look after themselves. Claude, the Australian, he sometimes helped a bit, fetched wood, that sort of thing, but your father couldn't, because of his mashed hand. So he was always writing, writing, writing. He wrote with his left hand then, but when he came back after the war he showed us how he had managed to write with his right hand again.'

I ask if the family of Amadeo Pafi still live in the village. She says no, old Amadeo died in the sixties, and his children have all moved to Rome. Amadeo had been largely instrumental in settling Dad and Claude in Vivaro.

After breakfast we were visited by a well-dressed young man wearing riding boots, whose name was Ermanno Pafi. He was a medical student from Rome and spoke a little French. His uncle, a man called Amadeo, was the village shopkeeper and one of Vivaro's leading personalities. Ermanno had been dispatched to give us notice of his uncle's impending visit.

I asked about Germans and Fascists. Ermanno confirmed our information that only a few Austrians were billeted in Vallinfreda, and they were 'pas tres mauvais'. Early in September the Germans had raided Vivaro. The raid had been a haphazard affair and a few British prisoners who were living there at the time had managed to slip out. Vivaro now looked after over thirty ex-prisoners, most of whom lived in casettas (small shacks) outside the village. Since the arrival of the Austrians in Vallinfreda, Vivaro had been left in peace. Consequently, these Austrians were quite popular.

As for the Fascist menace, Ermanno told us that amongst the six hundred odd inhabitants of the village, only five men had formerly been active supporters of the regime. All the families were closely interrelated. The five black sheep had been warned, in no uncertain terms, by their kinsmen (headed, we understood, by Amadeo Pafi) of what would happen to them when the English arrived, should they betray the prisoners to the Germans.

Presently Amadeo himself arrived. He was a strongly built, florid man, who looked like a well-to-do English farmer. He greeted us with much good will, but, as he spoke no French, I had to revert to my still rather inadequate Italian. I explained we were on our way to the front. He expostulated: we must not dream of going a yard further. He was in personal touch with the Committee of Liberation in Rome, which had given orders that all British prisoners must be stopped from attempting to cross the lines. The front was at present stabilised: the mountains were feet deep in snow and the people were starving. All the passes were closely guarded: Vivaro was as near to the front as we could get. We must go no further. I asked Claude, in English, what he thought of all this.

'Probably the usual Itie wind. All the same,' he went on, glancing outside at the steady grey drizzle, 'I wouldn't mind staying here until the weather clears. I could go for some more of those fried eggs.'

A little later in the day the escapers received their first visit from a resident prisoner:

There came a loud knock at the door.
'Chi è?' barked old Camilla sharply.

'Giovanni.'

The family relaxed. 'Entrate, Giovanni,' called Maria with a smile. The door opened and a figure advanced a trifle unsteadily into the room, a hand outstretched towards us.

'How do you do, sir, very pleased to meet you – and you, sir. You must excuse me, gentlemen, the fact is I've had a glass or two of wine . . .'

He was a South African. He was badly dressed and his complexion, in spite of the vino, was sallow. His husky, Cockney voice and his protruding lower lip reminded me of Gordon Harker. He was called John De Bere; the Italians had nicknamed him 'Giovanni matto' (mad John). His command of the language was fluent, if colloquial, and he had acquired the best Italian accent of any Britisher I have ever heard – an accomplishment I envied, for my own was execrable. The family seemed to regard him with amused affection. He teased them all incessantly and with great good humour, and made Angelo fetch some of his excellent wine.

Unfortunately, the vino had rendered him more or less incoherent. We were unable to glean much more information about the village than we had already, except that it did not lack alcoholic refreshment. Before he left, he promised that he would show us round the casettas where the other prisoners lived. They all came from Fara Sabina and most of them had been here since shortly after the Armistice.

'Ah, *Giovanni matto!*' Maria chuckles when I remind her of him. 'He was such fun, always made us laugh. He had such a nerve, that man. He had befriended the Austrians in Vallinfreda. Used to go and get drunk with them. That's why they left us alone: they liked Mad

John's company so much they didn't want him captured.'

'There was another man Dad liked a lot here – an old man called Mariano. He'd lived in the States for a while and liked to call everyone "son-of-a-bitch".'

'Yes, poor Mariano got into trouble in the end, after your father had gone. The Germans took to dressing up in civilian clothes, then testing people's loyalty. Of course, when they tried it on Mariano he gave them an earful about Fascists and Nazis, and sang the praises of the Americans. They locked him up for a year for his cheek.'

'Did you have a lot of trouble with spies?' I ask.

'Yes. There were quite a few of them, but we knew who they were. The families who didn't take in the prisoners, they were the ones we all suspected.' Again Maria stares out of the window at the distant horizon, as if looking back in time.

'What did you all think when Dad and Claude and Mad John disappeared?'

'We waited and waited for them. Mamma got more and more upset. Your dad told me they would be back in the evening, but they didn't show up. A couple of days later we heard some rumours about what had happened.'

Dad and Claude spent the whole of December in Vivaro, sharing a secret room with Mad John and another British prisoner. Maria's family continued to look after them but, as in Botto, the escapers grew bored and restless, especially when the weather set in and they couldn't even move around outside. Gradually they began to find reasons to go on expeditions to neighbouring villages – to scrounge a new pair of shoes, or dye for the uniformed prisoners' clothes, that sort of thing. When visiting the more distant villages they would sometimes stay overnight. If this was planned they invariably let Maria and Camilla know before they went.

At Christmas time there was a rash of rumours and scaremongering about imminent German raids, and a number of false alarms. One morning a German truck drove into the piazza, but its occupants were primarily intent on looting. Dad and Claude retired up the hill above the village, within sight but out of rifle range. From there they watched as the Germans chose the largest pig in the village and prodded it into the back of their truck. This provoked a mass slaughter of the rest of the village pigs, so determined were the people not to let their pork and bacon fall into enemy hands.

Christmas was a jolly affair with much wining and dining, which left the escapers stony broke. So, on 29 December 1943, Dad, Claude and Mad John decided to go on a foraging expedition to a village called Poggio Cinolfo, in the valley below, close to the small town of Carsoli, which was on the German defensive line from Rome to Pescara.

In the afternoon we dropped into the local for a glass of wine, and then continued our unsuccessful money scrounge. About 5 p.m. I suggested that we should give it up and go home.

'Might as well have one for the road,' said Claude.

'It's getting late,' I pointed out.

'We needn't stay long.'

We returned to the osteria, *which, at this hour, was crowded. I ordered a litre of white wine. A young man with long, black hair and a sallow complexion engaged me in* *conversation. He was an ex-*carabiniere. *I tried one of my usual opening gambits.*

'The Germans are plundering everything from Italy – grain, beasts, pigs . . .'

To my surprise, he interrupted: 'The Tedeschi *are all right; it is the Allies who are at fault.'*

I asked exactly what he meant.

'Oh, the English are not so bad, but the Americans are all villains – also the Australians.'

This remark somewhat naturally brought Claude into the conversation with a wallop.

'What's this long-haired bastard saying about the Australians?'

'He doesn't seem to like them.'

'If he'd like to repeat that remark,' said Claude with deliberation, 'I might feel like taking the matter up.'

But the carabiniere *evidently had no wish to pursue the matter, for he had edged his way outside the bar. Claude followed him.*

'I shouldn't start any arguments here,' I advised. 'These people don't seem very well-disposed towards us.'

'He'd better take back what he said.'

The young carab looked frightened. He explained that he had only made those provocative remarks to make sure we were really English. Of course he had not meant what he said: he thought we might be Germans. Claude accepted his apology, and he departed in rather a hurry.

We re-entered the bar to finish our drinks, which we had left on the counter. The wine was very light and we had drunk, between the three of us, only two litres. At Vivaro we often drank a couple of litres each, at one session, without feeling more than mildly happy. And I did not order any more.

From the moment when I picked up my glass, to the moment I came to, in a room full of screaming and gesticulating Italians, I remember nothing. Drugged wine, like the glass-eyed spy, sounds like something out of a yellow-backed 'penny dreadful'. Yet that is how it all happened.

. . . I noticed that the sallow young carabiniere was present. He was babbling Italian and pointing accusingly at Claude. I got to my feet and tried to push my way to the door. Two men seized me and hurled me back onto the chair.

Unlike drink, the effects of the dope, whatever it was, seemed to increase. I became only in part conscious of the general hubbub: it was like an interminable nightmare over which I had no control. Even when I looked up and saw that there were two German soldiers in the room, one of whom had his tommygun pointed directly at my stomach, I felt only a great weariness and apathy. I remember the swastika on his lapel – emblem of evil. Everything was finished. This time we should go to Germany – more prisons, more squalor, more boredom, perhaps worse. Tomorrow would be sheer hell, I realized that, but tonight all I wanted was to be left to sleep.

'We really didn't know what had happened to them, we had no idea,' Maria repeats. 'I wanted to go down to Poggio and ask about them, but Father said it wouldn't be sensible to go enquiring in a strange village about escaped prisoners. Then word came up to Vivaro that some Germans in civilian clothes, masquerading as POWs, had been arrested and taken away. We prayed that it wasn't them, that they had run away, not been taken. Papa was convinced that if they had fallen into German hands we would never see them again.'

I drive down to Poggio and easily locate the only bar in existence in the war. Its landlord is a young newcomer and knows nothing of those times. As I sip my undrugged wine an old man shuffles over to my table and begins confiding in a hoarse whisper: 'Fascists and spies, this village was crawling with them in the war ... full of Fascists and spies, bad people.' He looks round furtively, as if they might still be able to hear him. 'The woods were full of prisoners, prisoners everywhere, living in the *casetta*s, the sheep and donkey pens. The Germans got a lot of them. I remember seeing them being taken away in a truck, in their brown uniforms. Fascists and spies, there were so many then ...'

Back up in the mountains in Vivaro, I ask Maria about the people of Poggio. No, she says, they weren't renowned as bad people, but down there on the plain, close to the Germans in Carsoli, there were more spies and informants, as well as Fascist militiamen.

'Did you find Claudio to be an aggressive sort of person?' I ask. 'He seemed almost to want to fight the Italian who attacked him.'

'Yes, he was sometimes quick-tempered, but never with your father. He absolutely adored your father, would do anything for him. He had great respect for him, as he was older and of higher rank, I think.

'I never learned exactly what happened to them after they were taken in Poggio. Tell me about it, Osvaldo,' says Maria. My turn to take up the story, then, paraphrasing it from Dad's book.

The Germans took Dad, Claude and John to a transit camp just outside L'Aquila, about forty miles from Vivaro. There John, who was a sergeant, was separated from them. They never saw him again.

'What a shame,' Maria interjects. 'He was such fun. They must have missed his company.'

Two days later Dad, Claude and the other twenty or so officers were shipped a hundred miles further north, to a second camp where they were to wait for transport to Germany. Here, rather to his surprise, Dad turned out to be the Senior British Officer, obliged to liaise with Lieutenant Schreiter, the German camp commandant. However, this did nothing to dampen his determination to get out. On their third day there, Dad and Claude were out in the yard when they saw a German lorry drive in and unload sacks of bones for the prisoners' kitchen. A gaggle of prisoners surrounded the driver, hoping to trade Red Cross soap for cigarettes, while the prisoner kitchen crew unloaded the delivery. They then dropped the flap on the back of the truck, the driver got in and left the compound without being checked at the gate. He pulled up at the German lorry park, within the perimeter fence but outside the prisoners' compound.

It had to be worth a go.

They missed their first chance, so the kitchen sergeant-major put two of his sergeants in the back. They didn't get caught, but despite a clever attempt to cover for them their absence was detected at roll call the next day. Schreiter summoned Dad and asked him how the prisoners escaped. Dad said he had no idea. Schreiter guessed aloud that the men climbed the wire at the back of the compound, and ordered a working party to reinforce it.

The next day the bone truck came again and this time they were ready. Once the driver was distracted, Dad,

Claude and three other officers hopped into the back and lay down flat. They had already wrapped German blankets round their bodies, under their overcoats. Sure enough, the lorry reversed and turned, hurtled across the compound, past the guard at the gate, then pulled up in the Jerry transport park.

We lay there, still not daring to move. A breeze stirred a branch which brushed lightly against the canvas covering of the lorry. Lawlor drew in his breath: I think he thought it was me. Several Germans were about. We could hear their steps along the footpath, between the compound and their quarters.

My feet and hands felt like blocks of ice, although, thanks to the German blanket, my body was comparatively warm. I judged that the time must be about six o'clock: no one had a watch. We should hear the guard change at seven, and again at nine. We hoped to get away between nine and eleven.

I was relaxed and a trifle sleepy, when another lorry drove into the camp. Its headlights shone relentlessly into our truck, making us feel naked and revealed. It parked alongside our van. The driver got out, fiddled around outside, and even kicked one of our back tyres. An unpleasant moment, but somehow this evening I felt luck was with us. Sure enough, a minute later he departed.

At nine we heard the guard change.

'How about giving it a go?' whispered Claude.

The other three favoured another hour's wait. Perhaps it was as well they did, because a few Germans were still up and about. We could also hear the steady tramp of a sentry whose beat lay somewhere behind us. At nine-thirty the lights in the German quarters were extinguished. Claude raised his head cautiously to spy out the land.

'For Christ's sake keep down!' hissed Lawlor, whose nerves seemed a bit frayed.

'I've got to fix a route,' Claude answered. Then, after a pause: 'It's O.K. We'll have to watch two sentries: the guy behind, wherever he is (and he sounds bloody close), and the one on the bottom of the compound.'

We removed our boots. I tucked mine against my chest, inside my overcoat, and managed, with a struggle, to button it up. Claude had already slipped over the lorry on to the grass below. For a few seconds he had to wait, crouched against the back of the lorry, until No. 2 sentry started on his return beat.

Now that I could see outside, the night seemed hideously light and utterly still. Besides the lights from the compound and two powerful searchlights, a full moon cast its radiance over the whole camp. If the sentries could see us as easily as we could see them, Heaven help us.

Claude slipped away like a black wraith. He was making for the corner of one of the German huts, which cast a small square of shadow. He reached it, paused, and passed on; towards a shallow little gully which ran up the outside fence. His form was still plainly discernible from the lorry.

The others helped me out. Lawlor whispered some breath-less and incoherent instructions into my ear. I peered round the back of the van, but I couldn't spot him. Perhaps, after all, he was on the other side of the building, on the road. I waited until No. 2 turned his back on me, and then tiptoed off.

Certainly it was alarmingly light, but my stockinged feet made no sound on the hard ground. To my surprise, I found that I was actually enjoying this break. It was like an *exciting game of hide-and-seek. I thought of Schreiter's face on roll call next morning, and grinned to myself in the dark.*

The gully offered a little cover, but it was filled with old tins and rubbish. I had to pick my way with care. Once I knocked against something which rattled, and my heart stood still. Soon I spotted Claude: he was seated near the wire. A moment later I flopped down beside him. Instead of one fence, which we had expected, there were two. I wondered how I should cope with them. We had agreed that no one should start to climb until we had all arrived at the wire. Claude and I waited for several minutes.

'What the hell are they doing?' Claude whispered.

At last we saw them, but they seemed to be making for a point further up from where we were seated.

'You'd better start climbing, Ian,' advised Claude. 'With your crocked hand, you'll take longer than the rest of us.'

I gripped one of the wooden poles and put my foot on the bottom strand of wire, which gave forth a loud twang.

'Take it easy,' said Claude.

I continued to climb. The wire was taut and each strand seemed to twang more loudly that the last. I might just as well have started to play a banjo. The Germans must have heard. I felt like a monkey on a stick. And there was another of these infernal fences to climb. As I jumped down between the two, the wire gave forth a last shattering chord.

'Take the next one slower,' counselled Claude. 'But before you go, take the parcel.'

He hoisted it over to me and I tossed it across the second fence. I followed Claude's instructions and climbed the other more slowly. The twinging was perhaps a little less strident. Poor Claude! It was far worse for him than for me. I knew that, even if the searchlights were switched on to us, he would follow me. But miraculously all was still quiet. He hopped over, with considerably less noise, though the odd twang was unavoidable.

'Well, we've made it!' said Claude. 'Shake on that.'

Solemnly we shook hands. I could scarcely believe we were free again. It had all been so easy.

Avoiding all towns and villages, Dad and Claude spent the next three days walking high into the mountains, but still aiming for Vivaro. On the third evening a kindly Italian took them in, fed them and put them to bed in his shed. It contained a narrow couch and three bicycles. The minute they clapped eyes on the bikes, they both knew they wouldn't be able to resist. At about midnight, they sneaked off guiltily and cycled for the rest of the night. They soon realized that they were much less conspicuous mounted than on foot. Dad's height, for example, was not nearly as obvious on a bike. And who would expect escaped prisoners to be whizzing around on bicycles? They even took to riding through the towns, where several close encounters with Germans left them shaken but still at liberty. While it would have taken them weeks to return to Vivaro on foot, with the bikes it was a matter of days.

I drive out one sunny afternoon along the roads they took back to Vivaro. The Apennines are extremely barren and wild in this area and cycling uphill must have been impossible. Villages are few and far between, though I do manage to find the dam where Dad and Claude ran the gauntlet of Fascist sentries. They sailed past, waving politely, then had to dismount and push their way up the steep climb on the other side.

The lower ground is thickly wooded, with chestnut trees gleaming golden in the autumn sun. Several times I come upon people with mules and pack saddles, heading into the chestnut groves with large, strong sacks to gather the season's bounty.

CHAPTER FOURTEEN

*Shall I ever forget freewheeling down the long, curving hill
from Vallinfreda to Vivaro? Our troubles (very temporarily,
as it turned out) were over. The cool air fanned our tired and
perspiring bodies. In a few minutes we were going to savour
our salvation to the full. I longed to see old Camilla's face
light up with joy.*

*'I expect some of the others have taken over our room and
the beds,' I shouted to Claude.*

*'If it were Winston Churchill himself, he would go out on
his ear,' answered Claude.*

*As we turned the last corner, we passed a young Italian
from Vivaro who knew us by sight. At first he seemed to
doubt the evidence of his own eyes. He looked as if he had
seen two ghosts. Then his features creased into a broad grin,
'Bravo!' he yelled. 'Bravo!'*

We waved to him over our shoulders.

*Our reception was all that we had expected. I remember
that I clasped Camilla in my arms as I should have
embraced my mother. Her broad, noble features broke*

into a smile of incredulous joy.

'You have returned, my sons. Bravissimo!'

Within three minutes the whole village had heard, and half of it was gathered around Angelo's doorstep. Amadeo wrung us by the hand and asked innumerable questions. Maria had produced an enormous bottle of wine. Our bicycles were almost as much a centre of interest as ourselves.

Maria's eyes sparkle as she remembers the return of the prodigals, her knights in shining armour back from battle, having outwitted the enemy. She has insisted that I use her empty ground-floor apartment. So, sitting in the house where it all happened, I realize that some pretty deep heartstrings had sounded that day. When he embraced Camilla and Angelo as if they were his parents, Dad was responding to sensations that are more basic than those generated by being a fugitive on the run in enemy territory. I spent a couple of months continually on the move in Amazonia and by the end of it I desperately wanted to have somewhere I could think of as a base, a focus, a home. A place to return to, where you know you will be welcome. Vivaro clearly became 'home' for Dad, with his adopted parents, Angelo and Camilla. But some aspects of this 'home' were entirely new for Dad. I cast my mind back over his and his parents' lives.

My paternal grandmother, Joanna Bridge, was the daughter of a well-respected 'county' family of judges, bishops and the like. My grandfather, William Douglas Reid, was a doctor, a scoutmaster, artist and pillar of his small Scottish community; but he was not considered worthy of the hand of a daughter of the Bridges of

Harwich. When he asked for it, he was refused. So the couple eloped. Joanna was disowned by her natal family. Dad was born on 1 December 1915. By that time William had already served for a year in the trenches on the Western Front. He was killed, while tending the wounded, on 5 October 1917. Dad was not two years old. William, who had already received the MC for continuing to treat the wounded when wounded himself, received a bar to his MC posthumously. A letter of condolence arrived for Joanna from the King. This brave, decorated death was sufficient for the Bridges of Harwich to allow the errant Joanna and her infant son Ian to return to the family fold. So Dad grew up without a father, in a household that had once barred his parents from their door. In such a household, displays of parental affection were in any case extremely limited and certainly could not be matched by the easy, tender ways that Italian families, with their delight in 'little kindnesses', treat one another. So it was this pure joy at returning to the bosom of his surrogate family which so gripped Dad that day. I'd say that this was the sowing of the seed of his love for Italy as a whole: the rich and beautiful legacy of Camilla's and Angelo's love, a legacy that continues to pass on to the second and third generations of the Reid family.

Not that there was much time for any seeds of love to germinate in January 1944. Within a few hours of their return, word went round that German spies were in the village in plain clothes, recce-ing it for a raid. Dad and Claude retreated up the hill to the place where they had watched the Germans rustling the pig at Christmas time. The rest of that day, and the next, was quiet, but at four the following morning the escapers were woken by frantic knocks on their door and calls to run for it – the Germans had arrived in force.

'It was the seventeenth of January 1944. I have that date engraved on my soul for ever. The worst, most terrifying day of my life,' Maria declares solemnly. She too awoke to hear a neighbour bashing on the family door and calling up that the Germans had surrounded the village. Dad's book gives a lively rendering of the day from his point of view, but Maria has a very different version of events as they unfold, and she has had the rest of her life to piece together exactly what happened. She has much to tell me that Dad never knew.

'It all started when two brothers from our village set off very early to move some stock they had in the valley below,' she explains. 'At about four in the morning they heard a lot of truck engines revving up and they could see headlights and hear people shouting in German. They guessed what was going on and one of them raced back to the village to raise the alarm. They were cousins of Uncle Amadeo, good boys. One of them hammered on our door, knowing we often had prisoners here. It was about ten minutes before the Germans reached the piazza.'

So the Germans lost the element of surprise, slightly. Maria's brow tenses as she concentrates on giving me her version of the story.

'Mamma was ill in bed, very sick. Dad told us both to get dressed and he got up himself. At about that time a young married man, Mariano, bolted out of the village to warn the prisoners in the *casetta*s to go and hide in the woods. But he ran slap into the German cordon approaching the village. They challenged him, but he tried to sprint through. So they shot him dead, poor man. He had three small children, such pretty little babies.'

At the time when Mariano was shot, Dad and Claude were trying to break out of the village. Dad knew better than most what was likely to be going on, as he had commanded similar cordoned raids on villages in Palestine, flushing out terrorists in the 1930s.

We set off down the terraced hillside, making the best use we could of the cover afforded by sheds and vineyards. The shrill blast of a whistle, and the sound of guttural voices from below, brought us to a halt. I turned and saw that Claude had already started back up the hill, towards the village. I followed him. There was no point in running into the cordon which the Germans had obviously posted round the village. Climbing up the steep little terraces was harder work than jumping down them. The last could only be negotiated by scaling a walnut tree. With Claude's assistance, I managed. It is surprising how agile one becomes, with the threat of recapture to spur you on.

We were back where we started. Fortunately, Vivaro is a rabbit warren of a village, and the Germans had not yet found their way into our corner of it. But a few shots rang out from somewhere above us, and the people became more hysterical than ever.

'I wish the idiots would help us to climb on to a roof,' said Claude. 'It would be far the best plan.'

I tried to explain his idea, but they only gabbled and waved frantically towards the bottom of the village. Then I remembered that, outside our room, ran a small drain. We had considered its possibilities as a bolt-hole before, but had discarded it as being much too small for two. I reminded Claude of its existence.

'We'll never both get in there,' he said.

'It looks like we'll have to try,' I answered. 'They are bound to search all the stalls.'

Certainly that drain looked a most inadequate refuge. I wriggled myself in, head first, as far as I could, until my shoulders were firmly wedged between the narrow stone walls.

'That's as far as I can possibly get,' I called out to Claude.

'Good God! Then I'll never make it.'

He pushed his head and shoulders between my legs, but his feet were still sticking out. The woman who owned our room came to the rescue. She was a sensible and courageous old lady. She fetched some straw and threw it over Claude's feet. Some other onlookers, entering into the spirit of the thing, brought faggots and piled these on top.

'I hope they don't overdo the camouflage,' I whispered. 'It might look a bit suspicious.'

'If Jerry comes round the corner, we are certain to be caught,' said Claude gloomily.

'In fact the ladies covered them with brambles. They thought no German would imagine prisoners hiding under a pile of thorns,' Maria comments.

'Thorns? You mean blackberries, brambles? What on earth would they be doing in the middle of the village?' I ask.

'When they're dry, brambles burn at exactly the right temperature for baking bread. So we all had a pile of thorns outside our houses, next to the ovens. I had a long chat with the lady who hid them and she told me all about it after they had gone.'

Meanwhile, back at Maria's own house, the Germans smashed the door in with their rifle butts. They ordered everyone out, but old Angelo pleaded that Camilla be allowed to stay in bed as she was very ill. The German sergeant consented but ordered the old man and the two girls down to the village piazza, where all the villagers were being assembled while their houses were searched.

The piazza in Vivaro effectively breaks the village in half. Angelo's and Camilla's family houses and stalls were above the square, while Dad and Claude were lodging – now hiding – in a room below the square, in the 'rabbit warren'. You can't get from the lower to the upper village without crossing the square, the first place the German search party commandeered. So the Cerini family had no idea what was happening to Dad and Claude – and no way of finding out, at least initially.

'It was bitterly cold that morning, but we hardly noticed, we were so terrified. We didn't know what they would do with us, if they would take us away, or even just shoot us there in the square. After a few minutes the Germans started marching the escaped ones into the square. They lined them up on the other side from us. Then they screamed at us for the names of the people who had been sheltering them. In some cases the prisoners were actually caught in houses, so the Germans would demand that the householders step forward. They yelled at them and made them form a separate group. Poor Adeline, she was only sixteen, and she was soon sobbing. But I was older and I was determined not to lose control in front of Papa and the village.'

Maria's voice is quiet as the dreadful day replays itself in front of her eyes once again.

'I remember they called out one man, a neighbour who had in fact been looking after a couple of other prisoners. They said that they had received information, a list of suspect villagers, and his name was on it. "That's exactly what I would expect my enemies to do, to plant a list with you and get me shot. A very neat way to get rid of me, wouldn't you agree? But it is not true." He was allowed to rejoin us in the main group.'

'Were the Germans also looting as they searched?' I ask Maria.

'Good Lord, yes. We all had *cantine* in our houses, full with hams, vegetables, preserves and wine. They ordered us to open all the doors and they just helped themselves to all they could carry. If you refused to open the door they broke it down. One man tried to stop them, so they hit him on the head with a rifle. He came back to the piazza covered in blood.

'As it grew light, I noticed that one of the guards was paying a lot of attention to me. Every time I looked his way he was staring at me.' Maria giggles a little coquettishly. 'So I returned his gaze, gave him a little smile, played with him for a while. Then I made my way up to him and explained that Mamma was very sick in the house, and couldn't I and my little sister go and look after her? She needed us badly, I pleaded, looking up at him. All right, he said, you two girls can go, but your father stays here in the square. As we passed Papa, he whispered to me that I should go straight to my mother's room and get rid of all the clothes. "Take them out and bury them under the stones behind the chicken coop," he said.'

'Whose clothes were these?' I ask.

'Mamma's room was full of prisoners' clothes, some of them English battledress uniforms, which we were washing and dyeing and mending for them. If the Germans had got into my mother's room that morning we would certainly have been placed in the guilty group in the square.'

I pour a glass of the sweet fizzy wine that Maria has proffered and wait quietly for her to take up the story again.

'Once we had seen to Mamma and hidden the clothes, Adelina and I spent the rest of the morning dashing to and fro, glancing down into the square to see what was going on and if they'd caught your dad yet, but he never appeared. We were really pleased, but still very fearful for Papa.'

After an hour in that drain, I was beginning to wish we had taken a chance in one of the stalls. It was quite the most uncomfortable experience I have ever undergone. My ribs were squeezed so tight together that I could hardly breathe. A cold numbness spread from my right leg up the side of my body. We had nothing against which to rest our heads. I tried to persuade myself that to stick this out for a few hours was better than recapture: but as the morning dragged on, I believe that, had I been able to, I should have risked even that catastrophe for a ten-minute breather outside. I felt as if I had been caught in a pit accident and was slowly being suffocated to death.

Our old woman had not deserted us. Every hour or so, she would return and supply a sort of running commentary on the raid.

'They have caught about thirty prisoners. Most of them

tried to run out of the village . . . they have shot young
Mariano: he was frightened and tried to run away . . . they
have taken my husband to the piazza . . . they have arrested
the Podesta [mayor] *. . .'*

'What about Henry, signora? *Is he all right?'*
'Yes. They came into the stall where he was hiding, but
they did not find him.'

'Good! Thank you, signora. *Come back soon, won't you?'*
'Si, Capitano, poveri noi! Che disgrazia!'

'In the afternoon they released Papa and the other older
men, but they kept everyone else lined up down there, not
knowing if they were going to be killed, or taken away or
anything, for a very long time. I counted the prisoners:
there were thirty-two of them. At about four o'clock they
loaded all the prisoners into a lorry, then they loaded up
twenty men and one woman from the village. There was
a lot of yelling and screaming; everyone was absolutely
terrified. The priest went over to the German commander
and protested that a woman should not be taken away,
even though she had been caught in the same house as a
prisoner. The commander ignored him and ordered the
convoy to leave, though he did in fact release the woman
at Riofreda, at the bottom of the hill.'

'What happened to the rest of them?' I enquire gently.

'They were taken to a prison in Rome. They kept them
there for a few months, then they were released and they
came home. None of them was harmed, thank the Lord,'
she says.

Then, with a sigh, she tells me: 'It was the poor
prisoners, though, the poor prisoners who suffered. They
took them down to jail in Carsoli, and after a few days

they were all put on a train, taking them to a prison camp. It was spotted by an Allied fighter, who shot it to bits. They were all killed, I think. Perhaps one or two survived, but all the rest were killed by their own air force.'

A shiver runs down my spine. Dad was certainly within a hair's breadth of being on that train.

Periodically we heard the boom of an exploding grenade – not a pleasant sound.

'If they see this drain, they'll probably just drop one down and not bother to pull us out,' remarked Claude cheerfully. A messy death.

We were whispering together when we heard the tramp of heavy boots on the cobbled street below. The Germans entered the stall beneath us. For some moments they poked about amongst the straw, then we heard them emerge. But for some providential reason, they never came round our little corner. The afternoon wore on.

'Surely they must have finished by now,' I said to Claude. I had reached the stage when I harboured only one idea in my head, which was to get out of that wretched drain. My whole body felt paralysed.

'Better give it a bit longer,' Claude answered. 'Think of Bisignano [POW camp]*.'*

I reflected that if we hadn't stolen those bicycles, we should still be on our way back and should have missed all this. More poetic justice. Maybe honesty did pay sometimes.

At last everything seemed quiet outside and we risked emerging. Some women watched us anxiously, though they said the Germans had withdrawn their cordon. I asked whether Angelo Cerini had been arrested.

'No,' answered one of them. 'But they have taken away the brother of Amadeo Pafi.'

'And how many others?'

'Chi lo sa? The podesta and several more, they say. You know that they killed one man. You must leave the village at once, Capitano: it is no longer safe here.'

I sighed: 'Naturally, signora. We realise that.'

'It cheered us up a bit when a friend arrived in the evening with a note from your dad saying he and Claudio were still free. We realized of course that they would have to go now, but at least it was not to Germany. I saw a tear on Mamma's cheek as she cooked the pasta that evening, for just the four of us. Papa too was very quiet, staring into the fire and saying nothing. I suppose we were all relieved only one person had been killed, but we were shocked too, very shocked. The village was very quiet for the next few days.'

The light is fading as Maria finishes her tale, and I announce that I am going to take a walk round the village before the inevitable enormous supper Maria is sure to serve me. I amble down to the square. The old cripple is in his usual spot. He calls to me: 'Your dad, he was the really tall one, much bigger than you, wasn't he? Yes, I remember him now. He was the only *capitano* we had.'

'Were you here on the day of the raid?' I ask him.

'The day of the raid? Of course I was. They lined us up here, right where I'm sitting now. They held all the prisoners over there, under the tree.'

'Were you afraid of the Germans?'

'Afraid? Sure, I was afraid. We were all scared shitless,' he chuckles.

I stroll down into the 'rabbit warren', a maze of alleys and little passageways. Maria has given me the address of the room where Dad and Claude lodged. It's now a tidy garage-cum-storeroom. Outside it there is a manhole cover, presumably the entrance to the drain where they hid. Little lanes still lead to the terraced hillside below, though most of the cultivation has now ceased. I make my way back up across the square and climb to the top house in the village, which also belonged to Angelo. Immediately above it is the stall where the escapers stayed their first few nights in Vivaro. On the door is a light-green sign – VENDESI – For Sale. There is no lock on the door, just an iron bolt that slides free easily. Inside, a set of steps leads up to the hay loft. The floor there is very wonky so I decide not to risk walking on it. Below, the oxen stall, manger and water trough are just as they would have been when Dad and Claude flopped down here, exhausted, almost sixty years ago, after their night on the blasted heath.

Climbing further up the track above the village, I cast around for the spot where Dad and Claude watched the Germans pig-stealing below. From up here, only the rooftops are visible, so that the village looks much as it must have in the war. A clear evening, the sun is very low, casting long shadows across the valley below. Nestled in the nearby hills are all the little villages the escapers visited: Vallinfreda, Carsoli, Piétrasecca, Collalto and, below it, Poggio Cinolfo, where Dad and Claude were drugged and recaptured. I can picture all those adventures stretched out on the landscape below. And by visiting, seeing the sites, finding the players, feeling their moods, hearing their stories, it seems almost as if for a few moments they come back to life for me.

In the far distance, nearly out of sight in the fading light, I can just make out Tufo, the village they fled to after the raid on Vivaro.

CHAPTER FIFTEEN

ON THE LAST DAY OF THEIR CYCLE RIDE BACK TO VIVARO, Dad and Claude stayed the night in Tufo, about twenty kilometres short of 'home'. They knocked on the door of a house on the edge of the village and were taken in by a family called Di Marco. Actually, they were two families – two brothers who had divided the large house in half. Both families fed them handsomely and the escapers slept soundly in beds in the house. One of the two brothers had two charming and beautiful daughters, who spoke French, and were certainly a factor in Dad's and Claude's decision to head back to that particular village after the raid on Vivaro Romano.

As they approached, however, they met an old local, who suggested they leave the road at this point and make their way into a quiet valley on their left, where there were several prosperous and friendly farmsteads. The valley is about five kilometres outside Tufo, a tranquil backwater free of the dangers of village life. They decided to give it a try.

Tufo is an unusual village in that, though it does have a piazza, the day I arrive there it is deserted. No bench full of old boys idling the day away in the autumn sunshine, and no shops to enquire in either. I stroll round the village a bit and strike up a conversation with a man who was here during the war. I have the surnames of two village families: the Di Marcos and the Delfras. The Di Marcos are a wealthy family, he says; they lived in the big house right opposite the bar on the road up the hill. But both the brothers died long ago and, though they still have the house, the two remaining sons now live in Carsoli. It would be easy to find them, because they are important people in the small town and everyone know them. As for the Delfra family, the old ones are all dead and the only son has moved to Rome. I then ask him about the 'peaceful valley' where Dad and Claude were taken in, but I have only the Christian names of the family heads – Vincenzo and Erico. This draws a blank, so I thank him and walk back to my car.

Next stop the bar opposite the Di Marco house. The young but very helpful barman confirms that the Di Marco family own the house across the road and that the brothers now live in Carsoli. The older one, he says, has a *legnaia*, a timber business. As to the mysterious valley and its farmers, he too is uncertain. He is sure that his father-in-law, who is seventy-eight, knew all these people, but he is away visiting in Rome and won't be back until Monday (it is Friday). I should come back to see him then, but meantime, he explains, I have chosen an unfortunate day to visit, as the *castagni* are now ripe and all the *anziani* (old people) are off in the woods, gathering in their chestnut harvest.

I decide to head back down the road to search more carefully for the mysterious valley. In the middle of the village there is a hairpin bend on the main road and two old gaffers are chatting there, one on an ancient bicycle. When I try the list of names again, one of the old boys' faces suddenly lights up.

'Ettore, you mean Ettore's family. Yes, he had two or three sisters and his father was Vincenzo. Their surname, now, what is it? . . . Lustrati. That's it, they're called Lustrati. Vincenzo, the father, he's long dead, but his younger son, Ettore, he's alive. Go back down the road towards Carsoli for about five kilometres . . .'

At this point the other man interjects that it is four kilometres, not five. A furious row ensues, mostly in dialect, so I understand practically nothing except *kilometri*, *Dio buono* and *porca della Madonna!* – dire blasphemy indeed. Once the spat subsides I am told to go back *approximately* four and a half kilometres. After a steep drop I will cross a small bridge, then I'll see a house on the right. Not that one, but the next one is Ettore's house, old Vincenzo's place. Are you sure I don't need to turn off the main road, I ask. No, no, they insist that the house is right by the road.

So it seems that the 'peaceful valley', the secluded backwater, is now bisected by the main road. Bearing in mind my recent education on the twists and turns of modern road building with farmer Mario, I'm not entirely surprised.

Keeping a careful eye on the kilometre indicator, I roll back down the hill. Sure enough, after four and a half clicks I cross the bridge, pass the first house and pull up outside the second. I can see right away that it's deserted. Two long poles act as gates across the drive, and all the shutters are closed. There are three outer doors (I guess the house had been partitioned between the children after Vincenzo's death). I knock stoutly on each of them, to no avail.

Back up the road I can see an old man bent over, gathering weeds (rabbit fodder) from the bank. He is very friendly, and confirms that the house is Ettore's. He himself was a POW of the British when Dad was here, first in Libya, then later in England. He was treated very well and he likes the English. He confirms that until the 1960s this valley was very quiet, with only a mule track passing through it. But when the time came to build an asphalt road, it was decided it should follow the mule trail along the valley floor, rather than the original road, which ran along the other side of the ridge above us. He knows where Erico's house is too, though it's now abandoned, all the family either dead or living in Rome. He explains that some of the children come out from Rome and keep the land clear, maintaining the vineyard and the *orto*, the vegetable patch. Ettore will certainly be coming to-morrow, Saturday, as he will want to gather chestnuts for the winter, and maybe mushrooms too.

I drive back up to the village and drink another beer, this time in the company of a very animated old boy called Franco. He was about ten when Dad was here, and had been at school with Ettore. He didn't know Dad specific-ally – there were lots of prisoners here, he insists – but he did know two of the Italians who had befriended Dad here. One of them, Renzo Gulizia, 'had a little black beard like Lenin. I remember him well – a Communist through and through,' he says, chuckling. Renzo was a young and radical academic, who was effectively in exile here from

Rome. Dad took to him at their first meeting, about a month after the escapers arrived in 'peaceful valley'.

Life was pleasant, the weather mild and sunny throughout January 1944, and their only frustration was that there was no radio in 'peaceful valley'. Even this didn't bother them greatly, until rumours sped round the countryside of new Allied landings. One of them was said to be at Anzio, just south of Rome, only about seventy miles from Tufo.

Their host, Erico, was dead set against the escapers visiting Tufo, as he trusted the people of the valley to keep Dad's and Claude's presence a secret. He didn't trust the villagers. But with crazy stories circulating of the imminent fall of Rome and suchlike, Dad announced firmly that he must go to the village to hear a BBC News broadcast. He had already exchanged a few notes with the English-speaking 'professor' Renzo, and suggested they meet him in the village. Erico reluctantly agreed to escort them. Renzo was ill at the time.

I associate professors with wisdom and middle age. I was somewhat surprised, therefore, to find the man reclining in bed was no older than myself. (We learnt later that he was only twenty-one, but he looked a good deal older.) He wore a black beard, his eyes were a deep brown, and his features pale and rather finely chiselled. He had a gentle, courteous voice.

'Come in, my good friends,' he said. 'I am very pleased to see you.'

We shook hands, drew up chairs, and plunged into discussion of the news. The reported landing at Port Ostia was definitely untrue. A bridgehead had been established at

Anzio, but had not yet been greatly extended. I told Renzo that we seriously considered making our way to the front. He spoke against this scheme.

'There are three or four other prisoners who are living round here,' he informed us. 'When the Allies start their big advance for the liberation of Rome, I have promised to lead them across the mountains, along mule tracks, to Subiaco. From there it will be easy to strike west and join up with our forces. If you would get my map from that table over there, I will show you. I should be delighted if you would accompany us.'

We spread out the map on the bed and he outlined his scheme in further detail. It was well thought out and ingenious. Claude and I could see only one possible disadvantage. It seemed possible, though admittedly unlikely, that when the Germans were forced to withdraw from Cassino they might fight rearguard actions in these very hills, between Sora and Carsoli; in which case even the mule tracks might be dangerous. Ever since the news of the land-ings, I had been studying our little map and deliberating on the best course to follow. In the end I had come to the conclusion that the place where I should prefer to be situated, at the present moment, lay somewhere just north of Rome. When the Allies once reached the coastal plain, the enemy would have to abandon the capital and retire some distance north of it. All we should then need to do would be to lie low until the Germans had gone. Moreover, we should have none of the difficulties of trying to get through a stable front.

As we were talking, more visitors arrived to enquire after Renzo, amongst them two young students called Giovanni and Cesarino. Giovanni was a friend of Pepina's [their hostess] *whom we had met before. Cesarino, an earnest-looking young man, conversed with me in bad French, and seemed eager to make himself agreeable.*

In the bar, old Franco remembers Cesarino too, another student fugitive from Rome. Dad never mentioned his surname, but Franco knows it. It's easy to remember. Dall'Oglio, which phonetically means 'oily', or 'greasy'. Franco chuckles in a knowing sort of way about this Cesarino, but he's not sure what's become of him.

Dad and Claude talked over their meeting with Renzo and decided that they should make a move towards Rome. It wasn't simply that they wanted to place themselves better for the crossing of the lines. They knew that, by going into the village, they had compromised their security, and rumours of spies and imminent raids were now circulating in Tufo just as they had done in Vivaro days before the Germans came. They heard that a nearby village had been recently raided and half a dozen prisoners recaptured. While their presence had been virtually unknown a month ago, now many people from outside the valley knew they were there.

Their hosts, Erico and Pepina, and their neighbour Vincenzo all pleaded with them to stay, but they too recognized that things were not very secure. So they agreed that Dad and Claude should go away, at least for a while, and their hosts would put it about that they had departed.

They didn't last long. The weather turned bitterly cold and even on the plain the snow came up to their knees. They hoped to sneak into Vivaro to spend the night with

Angelo and Camilla, but before they reached the village they met a shepherd who told them that the Germans watched the place constantly and the people were terrified. So they trudged off to the outskirts of the neighbouring village of Collalto and scrounged a bed in a stall there. The next morning Claude was ill, with fever and nausea. Dad was afraid he might have jaundice, which had laid Dad out for a week before Christmas. They hung out for a further three days in the stall, and when Claude felt better they decided to return to 'peaceful valley'.

The reception on their return was not quite as warm as they were expecting. Sensing that Erico and Pepina were genuinely concerned about everyone's safety, Dad proposed that he and Claude should move out to some distant and concealed *casetta*. The idea was greeted with muted relief all round, and within a couple of days Vincenzo arranged for them to use part of a barn belonging to his neighbours, the Delfra family. The escapers stayed the night with Vincenzo before they moved in.

Early the following morning, he led us along a steep, twisting little footpath, up the terraced hillside on the west of the valley. About halfway up, where I paused for breath, one found oneself looking straight down over Vincenzo's land and the narrow valley. Here the path turned to the left along the side of the hill, with vineyards above and below. A hundred yards further on we were confronted by a stall.

'Here is your house!' announced Vincenzo.

I was surprised. We had expected to find one of the many little red-brick casettas, or sheds, which were scattered everywhere over the hillsides. This looked like an ordinary hay barn. A long narrow building, it was built upon a ledge below the crest of the hill. Above it, with the exception of one ploughed field, the ground was scrubby. Many small oak trees grew among bracken and bushes. Below, the vineyards descended in terraces to the valley.

Vincenzo produced an enormous key and unlocked a door at the end of the stall. We peered in. Three stone steps led down into a small spare room. An iron bedstead stood in one corner. There was one minute window, secured by a wooden shutter from inside, which Vincenzo opened. A narrow beam of sunlight streamed into the little chamber. I put my head out of the window. One got a splendid view over the Carsoli–Tufo road to the mountains beyond. In summer the place would be a dream.

At this juncture Erico appeared. He was carrying over his shoulders an immense mattress, which he had lugged, across country, all the way from his house. Rolled inside by a thoughtful Pepina were all the bedclothes, towels and linen we had been using, and several other odds and ends which she thought might prove useful. They busied themselves cleaning out the room, and widening the bedstead with the aid of wooden planks. As they finished, we observed toiling up the hill Vincenzo's three daughters, laden with crockery, cooking utensils, cutlery, a table, a chair, two stools made by their father, and heavens knows what else. Vincenzo had brought an axe and a billhook, and, while his family were setting things in order inside, he, Erico and Claude went off to cut fuel for our fire. The bare little room was transformed into as cosy a home as could be imagined.

'How do you like it?' asked Vincenzo.

'Magnifico,' I declared. 'We shall be very happy here. You couldn't have done better.'

'And you will not mind cutting your own wood?'
enquired Erico anxiously.

*Claude assured him that on the contrary he would be glad
to have something to occupy him. They looked pleased and
relieved.*

*In truth, both Claude and I were delighted with 'Casa
Nostra', our new home. We felt we should be as secure here
as it was possible to be anywhere. The place was at least
three miles from any village and was therefore most unlikely
to be included in any German raid. It was well off any
beaten track, and looked even less 'inhabited' than the
numerous casettas. Besides which, the two families had done
everything in their power to make us comfortable. They had
forgotten nothing: even a table cloth and a soap dish had
been provided. And, finally, fond as we were of Erico and his
family, we looked forward to our future independence.*

The next few weeks were the happiest and most secure
Dad spent in all his time on the run. The two of them
clearly enjoyed playing 'house', keeping it tidy and clean,
absorbing themselves in domestic trivia like washing-up
and dusting. Though the food supply from the farms
below was a bit erratic, the owner of the barn, old Delfra,
brought them up a huge sack of potatoes for the leaner
times or when the weather set in. Dad nicknamed the old
boy 'Good-time Charlie', and became adept at baking the
potatoes in the ashes of their fire, a skill he later passed on
to us kids when we had bonfires at home in England.

Every autumn we made big fires to burn up the fallen
leaves, and Dad could never resist sending one of us
children back to the house to fetch a few potatoes, which
he placed carefully where they would cook slowly,

without burning. Then we all just stood around staring at the flames, our cheeks glowing. Dad often put his hands round our shoulders and we peered up at his glowing, smiling face. When they were done, Dad took a garden fork and raked them out of the embers. We picked them up, yelping at the heat and tossing them from hand to hand. Once they were cool enough we guzzled their delicious flesh and crunchy, ashy skins.

Most days, old 'Good-time Charlie' Delfra came up to *Casa Nostra* to collect fodder for his animals from the barn, and would stop for a chat and a glass of wine. Vincenzo's children – Ettore and the two older girls – scampered up and down the path from their farm, bringing bowls of pasta and snippets of gossip or news, mostly unreliable. One day, in the middle of a blizzard, three very respectable middle-aged ladies paid a call, bringing gifts of butter and a rabbit's haunch, welcome additions to the baked potatoes. The students Giovanni and Cesarino also visited quite often. All these diversions distracted the escapers a little from the restlessness and boredom that continued to gnaw at them. Then one day Renzo dropped by.

Renzo had recently made several journeys to and from Rome, in connection with the Committee of National Liberation. On returning from his latest trip he came down to our shack to see us. He had some important business to discuss. The Committee had decided to organise small armed bands, each consisting of ten or twelve men, all over occupied Italy. Renzo had been entrusted with the formation of one such band and was now busy enlisting recruits.

'I wondered if you would like to join me,' he said.

I asked if he had approached any of the other prisoners. He said he had contacted all of them, but only two, an Englishman and a South African whom we had not yet met, had accepted his invitation. The rest, including Chris, Sammy and 'the Doctor', had turned him down.

'What weapons have you got?' Claude asked.

'So far only some bombs and some ammunition, but I hope to obtain some rifles from Carsoli in one or two days. I have the bombs with me.' He indicated his haversack. 'If you will permit, I will leave them here with you.'

I parked the haversack on one of our shelves.

They signed up to Renzo's Partisan group, though of course no actions could be planned until sufficient arms had been gathered. In the meantime, the two of them took to visiting the village when the weather was clement. They didn't feel their safety was compromised, because few people now knew where their *casetta* was, and if asked where they were living they just said 'in the countryside'. There was an open invitation to eat at the Di Marco and Delfra family tables, and there were several radios. Cesarino even organized occasional musical evenings.

Cesarino, the student whom we had met at Renzo's bedside, was one of the most anxious to be on good terms with us and was always coming down to see us and inviting us to his rooms. He was a serious-minded young man and a devout Catholic. I got the impression that he disapproved, when he learnt that Claude and I were Socialists. He described himself as 'a democrat, but not a Communist.'

We found him useful for several reasons. Firstly, the

*woman in whose house he lodged possessed a wireless.
Secondly, he lent me some books, including an
Italian–English grammar and some French novels. And,
thirdly, he was the centre of a musical set of young people,
who gave periodic impromptu concerts in his rooms.
Cesarino himself played the accordion (rather indifferently),
but amongst his friends was a piano teacher of decided
talent, and another young man who played the violin. Not
having heard any music for months – up till now I had
found the Italians a disappointingly unmusical race – I
looked forward to these soirées. I noticed that Renzo was
never present.*

*One afternoon, after the young pianist had entertained us
with some Chopin and Debussy, Cesarino drew me aside and
asked whether it was true that we had joined Renzo's armed
band.*

'Why do you want to know?' I enquired.

*'Well, you see,' he explained, 'we students are keen to help
him too, but he has not asked for our assistance.'*

*'I have no idea why that is,' I said, truthfully
noncommittal.*

*. . . A few days later we saw Renzo. I told him, casually, that
I believed Cesarino and some of the students were anxious to
join the band. Renzo looked uneasy.*

'You don't much like Cesarino, do you?' I said.

*'I will explain,' said Renzo. 'When I came here shortly
after the Armistice, Cesarino was still a bit of a Fascist. You
know that he is a great Catholic and very frightened of
Communism. When I first arrived here, I had some difficulty
in finding anywhere to live. Now, of course, the people trust
me and it is different. But, then, I sometimes found it hard*

even to get food. Once I asked Cesarino to sell me something
to eat. He offered to lend me a loaf of bread. That is why I
am not anxious to have much to do with him.'

After that, we too avoided Cesarino as much as we could.

When I drive in to Tufo the next day – Saturday –
Ettore's gate is still barred, the place deserted. So I go on
up to the village, where the friendly barman confirms that
Ettore will almost certainly show up today to gather
castagni. On my return down the hill to the farm, the bars
are down and a white Fiat Punto stands in the drive.
Attached to it is a small trailer, containing two large sacks
full of chestnuts. Two sets of shutters are open on one side
of the house, but apart from that there is no sign of life. I
walk around banging on doors, then decide to check two
large sheds on the far side of his vegetable patch, at the
foot of the steep, wooded hill.

Though there is nobody there, as I approach the sheds
I can hear an animated conversation from within the
woods. Two men emerge, both with large baskets full of
mushrooms.

A small man with large, thick glasses grasps my hand –
Ettore, Vincenzo's youngest son. As soon as I finish my
standard introductory speech he says: 'You must be
Gianni's son, I suppose.' He speaks in such a matter-of-
fact way that it rather surprises me: it's as if ghosts from
his childhood constantly reappear here. This is so different from the emotionally charged greetings from Maria in
Vivaro and Adriana in Botto. We chat on the way back to
the house. He was about ten when Dad was here, and of
course he remembers him well – 'he ate dinner with us
practically every night for several months.'

'He used to joke with us kids, and we would take milk and food up to the *casetta* for them. We took everything up there for them, your Dad and the shorter one – Claudio, I think.'

I am dying to see *Casa Nostra* – Dad's and Claude's home for so long – so I ask him where it is. He points to the ridge high above the valley floor. In the war the whole of that hillside was vineyards, he explains. The hut was at the very top, where the woods had started then. I know this from Dad's book. But the hillside had been abandoned for years and the hut is now totally overgrown, covered in brambles, impossible to reach, he says. I feel crestfallen. But I've seen sufficient numbers of totally overgrown buildings in rural Italy to know that Ettore is probably right.

Offering the usual glass of wine, he leads me through the room that was the family kitchen, where Dad ate. We talk of the war and of Dad's visit with Mum afterwards – they were all so amazed and pleased that he had survived. Then he mentions that there is one other old man in the village, called Irminio, who knew Dad in the war, whom I should talk to. He draws me a little map and I set off to try to find him. His house is tight shut. As I drive back out of the village I can't put the thought of *Casa Nostra* out of my mind. Though these abandoned buildings can get very overgrown, I have often been with Marcello on our farm as he expertly cut his way through seemingly impenetrable bramble thickets to show me something of interest. Ettore was born and brought up on this farm and has always collected wood, chestnuts and mushrooms from the land. As I reach his house I see his car is still parked outside. He and his friend are loading logs into the trailer, so I stop. Out of politeness he's already said that we could try to get through to *Casa Nostra* if I really want to, so after we've filled the trailer I broach the subject again. Ettore assents without hesitation.

As I set off behind him I suddenly feel Dad's presence. This little chap, though then somewhat smaller and younger, accompanied Dad up and down this very path countless times. At first the path is easy – Ettore cleared it a few years ago to bring wood down from the hill. But the clearing ends abruptly and we are suddenly in the thick of it, Ettore wielding his billhook adroitly at brambles and bushes. He stops briefly to cut a forked stick, which he uses to push the brambles to one side or flatten them onto the ground, clearing a little tunnel for us to squeeze through. Eventually we come to a real thicket, which looks totally impenetrable. I suggest we skirt uphill of it, then work our way back onto the (totally invisible) path. This strategy works, though the slope is so steep that we have to pull ourselves from trunk to trunk as we climb. On the way Ettore notes several clumps of *funghi*, which we will collect on the way down. He points to the terraces too, their walls just visible beneath the thick undergrowth. In Dad's time this was a vineyard. Now wild boar, bramble and hazel thicket prevail.

Eventually the path levels out and the undergrowth thins. In front of us there is a rough stone wall, the top of the barn, with roof and side walls sloping downhill away from us. A door in the centre creaks open to reveal a large empty hay loft. To the right three stone steps lead down to a large room with a window on the opposite, downhill side. *Casa Nostra*. The roof above the window has caved in, as has about half of the floor. A wooden tub, once worn on the back for collecting grapes, is half embedded in the broken floor. In the corner nearest the door, the wall is smudged all the way to the ceiling with soot.

'That's where they had their fire: there is no *camino*, no chimney. Their bed was over there by the window and they kept the table and chairs here, by the fire. It was cosy and snug in here, very clean and tidy. They were proud of it,' Ettore explained in a quiet voice.

I sit on the step and look and breathe and smell and touch the nearly gone place. To anyone but Ettore and me, it is just another half-collapsed hut on an abandoned hillside. But we know it was once a refuge, home for a desperate but loved pair of human beings. Flames dance on the walls and light filters through the roof tiles; Dad's mashed hand carefully places a potato in the embers; an old man, unshaven, with few teeth, garlic breath and a wrinkled smiling face, holds up his wine glass in salute; then the darkness descends.

CHAPTER SIXTEEN

On that morning, April 6th, by a strange coincidence the anniversary of my original date of capture in Africa, I awoke, as I generally did, soon after dawn. Through the slit in the roof above my head I could see blue sky. Claude was still asleep.

There came a knock at our door. I thought one of Vincenzo's kids had brought us some milk, but when I opened the door Vincenzo himself was outside. He looked excited and upset. Clearly something was wrong. He spoke quickly, in a half-whisper.

'You must get out at once. The Tedeschi are making a raid on Tufo.'

Dad and Claude were not overly concerned. They were miles outside the Germans' cordon and their hut commanded views of the main Carsoli–Tufo road and the mule track in the valley, as well as the only path up to the hut. Vincenzo offered them food for the day, so they went down to his farm and picked it up. They decided it might be best to clear off for a couple of days while things cooled down.

'I suppose we'd better plant those grenades somewhere before we leave,' I said.

During the next few seconds I experienced exactly the same sensation as I had felt with Tom on that morning of October 4th last year. The catastrophe was just as sudden and just as utterly unexpected. A stampede of feet from behind the stall, a glitter of weapons, and the same guttural shouts.

'Hände hoch! Hände hoch!'

For me the same bewilderment, temporarily annihilating fear. As we struggled to our feet I made an effort to pull myself together. There were eight Germans, with a Major who spoke English in command.

'You are a Captain,' he announced, addressing Claude.

Claude looked furious. He scowled:

'No, I'm not.'

The Major turned to me: 'Then you are the Hauptmann.'

'Yes. You are right this time,' I admitted.

Questions were chasing one another helter-skelter through my brain. How in heaven's name did they get here? They couldn't have come along a track or even a path, because there wasn't one. Over the hill, then? But why choose this shack out of the hundreds that littered the mountainside? And how on earth did he know that one of us was a captain? Even then, the possibility of treachery never occurred to me.

'Well, now we shall go and drink a little of your wine,' said the Major, when we had been searched. 'Oh yes,' he went on sarcastically, 'we know you have wine in your house. The Italians bring it to you, don't they? They look after you pretty well, I think.'

I supposed that, before surprising us, they had peeped into our room and observed on the floor our old *vino* flasks, which we used for carrying water. I was glad that in actual fact we had no wine on hand, but I thought it as well to humour the man.

'We should be delighted to offer you some wine if we had any, Major,' I answered, 'but I am afraid we have only water.'

We were escorted inside. The Major picked up the flask, found my statement correct and poured himself out some water. Beads of perspiration glistened on his brow. He must have had a long climb over the hill.

Two more Germans arrived and stood outside the door. I gave them a casual glance. The face of one seemed vaguely familiar. I looked at him again. I could hardly believe my eyes. It was Cesarino. He was wearing a German tin hat and greatcoat over his civilian clothes. So that explained it. Cesarino had led the Germans to our hut.

I turned excitedly to Claude. From where he was standing, he couldn't see outside.

'Look!' I cried. 'Do you see who's outside? It's—'
'Shut up!' interrupted the German Major.

But I was so excited that I had almost forgotten we were prisoners. Nothing short of a bullet could have stopped me telling Claude.

'It's that wretch, Cesarino,' I said.

'Shut up!' yelled the German Major again. 'And sit down on that bed!'

I remembered where I was and sat down. The Major smiled – an unpleasant smile.

'Yes, you see your old friend was a little Badoglio after all.'

He was plainly as contemptuous of 'traitors' as we were. I looked him in the face and smiled ruefully back.

'You win,' I said.

I knew that whatever action he chose to take, he had more respect for us than for the cowering Italian outside. He gave an order to an N.C.O., who marched Cesarino away.

It was only then that the full significance of these events struck me. And when it did I had a moment of blind panic. Renzo . . . the armed band . . . the grenades at this very minute reposing on the shelf above my head . . . prisoners had been shot out of hand, merely for carrying a pistol . . . an icy fear laid hold of me, the fear of sudden and violent death.

'You've got to have a story ready,' I said to myself. 'You've got to think. Faster than you ever thought in your life.'

The point was: how much had Cesarino given away? And how much did he know about Renzo and our ridiculous armed band, anyway? I remembered that conversation in which he'd complained about not being allowed to join. But had I committed myself as to our share in it? I didn't think so, but . . .

'Have you any arms here?' demanded the German Major, as if reading my thoughts.

There was no point in saying we hadn't. They were bound to search the place. 'Well, here goes,' I said to myself.

'Yes, there's a bag of Italian crackers in that haversack.' With a casual gesture I indicated the shelf. 'They've been here for weeks. I've no idea how they work or whether they are primed.'

One of the Germans lifted down the haversack, and put it on the table. The Major extracted one of the grenades. It was of the type which the Eighth Army nicknamed 'Red Devils'.

'And where did you get these?'

'Oh, we've had them for ages,' I answered, as if they were uninteresting and quite unimportant. 'One day, when we were in the village, an Italian asked us to keep them for him. He had given us some food, so we didn't like to refuse. Anyway it was no trouble to us to keep them here.'

'And who was this Italian?'

I shrugged my shoulders.

'I haven't the faintest idea. We'd never seen him before and we've never seen him since. I suppose he was merely passing through. As a matter of fact, I'd forgotten all about the things until you mentioned the subject of arms.'

The Major emptied the contents of the haversack on to the table. On top of the grenades cascaded a shower of small arms ammunition. I had forgotten about this. Thank God the rifles hadn't arrived from Carsoli, anyway.

The Major gave a curt order to the two Germans by the door, upon which they drew their pistols. Then he turned to me with his sinister smile.

'So your little fight against Germany is over.'

I felt myself grow hot and cold, but for once my brain worked fast.

'Look here, Major,' I said, 'you are a fighting soldier, aren't you?' Was it my imagination, or did he bridle slightly? 'You must know these Italian grenades. Once in Africa one of them exploded practically at my feet: it didn't even wound me. If you imagine that we should be so stupid as to attack anybody when armed only with a bag of these children's crackers, then you are not such an intelligent man as I think you are. As for that ammunition, what good is it to us without anything to fire it out of? You can turn this place upside down, but you will find no rifles here.'

He looked at me quizzically for a moment.

235

'So,' he said. 'Well, first we will have a cigarette.'

He sat down facing us and offered his cigarette case. I heard Claude utter a sigh of satisfaction as he inhaled great lungfuls of smoke. But a phrase from some stupid thriller kept running through my head! 'The condemned men were allowed to smoke a cigarette before they were shot.' The Germans in the doorway still had their pistols at the ready. The Major's face wore the same cynical, half-amused expression. I could imagine his ordering our summary execution in exactly the same tone that he had offered us a cigarette.

'Is this really the end of all things?' I thought. 'Outside the sun is shining on the valley. Is this the last time we shall see it?' I wondered if I could keep up a pose of unconcern to the end. It was an intolerable strain, but I thought I could, because the whole situation was so nightmarish and fantastic that I only half-believed it myself. One read about things like this, but they didn't really happen. My real self no longer inhabited my body. It was looking on from somewhere just above my head. My body was playing a complicated part, which bore no real relation to myself. It would go on doing so for as long as I told it to. No, this business of dying well would not be nearly as difficult as people imagined. My respect for the aristos of the French Revolution diminished considerably.

All the time that these thoughts were running through my head, I was forcing myself to talk. The longer we could keep the Major engaged in light-hearted banter the less opportunity he had for asking awkward questions and the less chance there was of him having us shot in cold blood. Or so I reasoned. I wanted him to get the impression of a good-natured, stupid, slightly fatuous British officer. I pointed to

236

the picture of two blonde bathing girls we had cut out of a
Jerry magazine and pasted on the wall above our bed . . .

. . . At length the Major led the conversation back to more
immediate concerns, and intimated that it was time for us to
depart. I asked if I might first collect some of our small
possessions such as washing things and soap. He had no
objection.

'But you will find much better soap in Germany,' he
pointed out.

A great wave of relief swept over me. We were going to
Germany. We were not going to be summarily shot.
Afterwards, Claude told me that he experienced exactly the
same sensation of relief. He too was convinced that we were
for it this time.

As we've come all this way, deep into the woods, Ettore
murmurs that he is going to take a look around for *funghi*.
He leaves me sitting on the stone step of *Casa Nostra*. The
enormity of the events that took place here rings in my
ears: the betrayal, the sheer terror of the drawn guns, the
interrogation, so frightening that Dad had a sort of out-
of-body experience, normally associated with near-death
experiences in traumatic conditions. Though he was fully
conscious, this was indeed an experience on the brink of
death. It was also the sort of appalling shock to the system,
like Tom's death, that can generate long-term psycho-
logical problems. Most certainly it was 'traumatic stress' of
a particularly vicious type.

Above all, though, as I sit here I realize how humiliat-
ing the whole thing – not just this episode, but the entire
business of being a soldier-turned-escaper, disarmed and
on the run – must have been. Here Dad saved his

and Claude's lives with his wits. The Germans routinely executed prisoners caught with weapons. But for a soldier, dealing with betrayal and capture without any means of redress must have bitten deep into him. Here, his only recourse was to play 'poor Tom's a-cold', Lear's fool, in a desperate bid to save their lives.

Perhaps, for Dad, the betrayal was the worst thing. He had counted Cesarino a friend, despite Renzo's reservations. More to the point, Cesarino was an Italian who had clearly declared himself on the side of the anti-Fascist, anti-German, pro-Partisan, pro-Allied POWs faction. Soon after his recapture Dad asked himself a whole set of questions about why Cesarino had done this, but he couldn't find the answer. It was as if the one thing Dad had come to trust and love – the goodness of the Italian people as a whole – had suddenly disintegrated in front of him.

I realize here, in *Casa Nostra*, that I have come to a turning point, a moment in Dad's life where something went out of him, for a very long time. In part it was innocence, perhaps even naïvety. In part it was his *joie de vivre*. It was the third occasion he'd been caught in six months, this time in by far the most menacing circumstances. It took the sparkle away, obliterated the sense of adventure that had sustained him so well up until then. After this betrayal and recapture, the texture of his book changes. Though he did in fact escape twice more, the drive was gone, the sense of adventure much less easily kindled. He had grown mightily weary of being on the run, of this constant dice with death, where all the odds are stacked against the escapers and all the protections that give soldiers some sense of safety, self-preservation, are denied them.

Ettore comes back to the hut with his jersey off, its arms tied up and stuffed into its neck, the torso now half full of mushrooms. On the way back down the hill we fill the rest of it.

Back at the farmhouse, Ettore fetches a wine bottle and we sip his light, pinkish wine. I ask him if he has any idea why Cesarino betrayed Dad.

'I'm not sure exactly why, but the Germans forced him to betray them, I know that. They threatened to kill him if he didn't take them to the hut. He didn't want to, but they forced him. They didn't pay him, they made him take them there. We were all very upset that someone we knew, who had eaten in our house, should do such a thing, but my father said he was certainly forced to do it.'

'In his book, Dad says he was taken back to the village with Cesarino, who was extremely miserable. There Dad was put with some other British POWs who had also been caught in the raid. They said that earlier they had seen the Germans roughing up Cesarino, then putting a helmet and greatcoat on him and driving away with him. That must have been when he led them up to the hut,' I muse. 'But I still don't understand why he did it and how the Germans knew that he knew where to find them.'

'You could always ask him, you know,' Ettore says, quite calmly. 'He's still alive. He lives somewhere near L'Aquila, somewhere like Rocca Media, I think.'

For a moment I can't speak, I'm so dumbfounded. My turn for the cold sweat now. Cesarino, the traitor, alive and well seventeen years after Dad's death?

Ettore continues: 'He was a lawyer, but he's retired now. I see him occasionally. You know, he once told me that he had some of your dad's diaries, which were confiscated after the arrest. He said he still had them, but that was a long time ago.'

That settles it. I'll have to try to find him.

CHAPTER SEVENTEEN

DRIVING BACK TO MARIA'S HOUSE, I FEEL FUNDA-
mentally confused. It never occurred to me that I might
uncover any of the villains of the piece, such as Schreiter,
and now I face the certain knowledge of Cesarino's continued existence. What should I do? Should I confront
him or should I turn my back and walk away? Strong
impulses draw me in both directions at the same time. I'll
sleep on it, take my decision in the morning. First, though,
I need to go back very carefully over Dad's descriptions of
the events immediately after he and Claude were caught.
I can remember that Cesarino's treatment after the raid
seemed very ambiguous. I also remember that Dad's
diaries, by then swollen to six notebooks, were discovered
and confiscated at that time.

One of the recaptured prisoners saw Cesarino in the
village square prior to Dad's recapture. He told Dad:

*'Cesarino looked scared stiff. I think they threatened to beat
him up: it looked as though they had something on him.*

Then they made him put on a German greatcoat and tin hat, and drove him off.'

Dad speculates:

I found it difficult to believe that he would ever have set out to betray us gratuitously, and with malice aforethought. At the same time, I very much doubted whether he would be likely to offer much resistance to German pressure at a possible cost to his own skin. If the Germans had tackled him, he might have given us away out of sheer fright. The question would then arise, however, why should they have tackled him? Was it just bad luck? Or had they been put up to it by someone who knew as much as Cesarino knew, and had no scruples in turning his knowledge to account? We could not tell, and probably should never know. Perhaps it did not matter much, for in one way or another the harm had already been done.

Later that day Dad, Claude and the other captured prisoners were loaded into a German lorry, along with some of the locals who had also been arrested. Then Cesarino was marched out, evidently under semi-arrest, between two German soldiers and put into the same truck as the prisoners. They were then all driven to the major's headquarters in Avezzano, about thirty kilometres away. There the Italians were separated from the British and there was no further mention of Cesarino. But that same evening a German guard saw Dad trying to hide his diaries, prior to being searched and interrogated. He confiscated them. After the interrogation Dad asked for them back and the Germans agreed to return them. But he never saw them, or Cesarino, again. However, Cesarino was certainly in the vicinity when they were taken and, very probably, thrown away by the Germans.

After a restless night, tossing and turning, wondering what to do about this new turn of events, my tracker instincts get the better of me. It takes a little over an hour to reach L'Aquila, a large town sprawled over an upland plain in the Apennines. It's Sunday morning, so I stop at a newsagent's and ask to borrow the phone directory. A brief chat with the stall-holder establishes that there is a village called Rocca di Mezzo, and there, sure enough, is listed: Dall'Oglio Cesare Dr.

The village is high in the mountains, a place of clean, fresh air in the summer and skiing in the winter, the newsagent tells me, and she comes outside to point me to the right road. Half an hour later I find that, even though it's Sunday, the grocery in the village square at Rocca di Mezzo is open. The *padroni* cheerfully give me directions to his house, but say that though he was here last weekend they haven't seen him or his family this weekend. Sure enough, when I get to his smart apartment block, I am hailed by the caretaker, who tells me that Dr Cesare is not here. 'But look him up in the Rome phone book. You'll find two Dall'Oglios listed. Him and his son, they both live in Rome.' I thank her and depart. My heart has been thumping ever since I reached Rocca di Mezzo.

Even as she fetches the Rome phone book, Maria counsels me to leave him alone. Hers is the voice of compassion, of reconciliation. Though factionalism remains a constant in Italian life, I have heard from Maria and many others that, once the war was over, there was a need to draw a line under the past, start afresh, bury the differences and the negative experiences. I follow this line of thought and sympathize with it, but then a wave of anger rolls through me. This prosperous lawyer deceived my father into thinking he was a friend. His actions led directly to Dad spending a further year in vile, stinking prisons in Italy and Germany. That extra year ate away at his soul and maybe even shortened his life. If Cesarino hadn't betrayed Dad and Claude in April 1944, they would almost certainly have been liberated by the Allied advance just a few weeks later. So why did he do it? Now that I know that I *can* ask that question, I feel I must.

I find his number in the book and call him.

A frail, elderly female voice answers; I ask to speak to Dr Cesare, explaining that I am English and my father was a friend of his during the war. He comes on the line. His voice is hesitant – he's uncertain whom he is speaking to – but perfectly composed. He tells me immediately that he can't remember much about that period of the war, his memory is not clear. He asks, 'Was it you who was there in 1944?' and I reply no, it was Dad. He sounds relieved, but again protests that he cannot remember anyone called Gianni or Giovanni, nor any British captain by that name.

'Are you telling me that you cannot remember any of the events of the sixth of April 1944?' I ask pointedly.

There is a long silence, a more than pregnant pause. Then I hear a sigh, before he says slowly: 'Yes, I do remember some of the things that happened that day. But you know that everything was extremely confused in those times. You know, you should take this up with our National History Committee. Why don't you talk to them, as they are reviewing this entire period?'

'No, no, *dottore*, what we are talking about here is nothing to do with National History Committees. What we are talking about is that it was you who led the Germans to the *casetta* where my father was hiding. He saw you there, in German uniform. These are not issues to dispute, these are the known facts. I know all about it: he wrote a book about it after the war. That's what we are talking about here.'

'Ah, yes, your father. He was some sort of journalist, was he? Yes, I do remember some journalist among the British prisoners. He was a newspaper man, wasn't he?'

I quickly close off that line of retreat. 'No, *dottore*, my father was a professional soldier, a regular army officer since 1936, not a reporter, though he did keep a diary. The man who told me about you, Ettore Lustrati, said you had kept some of Dad's writing. Is that correct?'

'Ettore? Who is this Ettore? I don't think I know him. Diaries? Yes, there were some books in English, but it was all so long ago. I have no idea where they are now.'

Another long silence, so long that I ask him if he is still there.

'I wonder if you would allow me to come to visit you, in Rome. We have Dad's side of the story, published in his book in 1947, but I'd really like to hear your version of what happened, so that we can all understand our history a bit better. I know that this all took place a very long time ago, in a very confused period, but I'd still like to hear your account.'

'I am very ill at present, very sick. I don't have a clear recollection of those times, not clear at all. How long are you here for? Maybe I could see you the week after next?'

I say I will be gone by then.

'Well, I am very busy tomorrow, but you could try calling me late on Tuesday morning and we'll see if we can meet later in the week . . .'

At this point the frail female voice comes back on the line. I have the distinct feeling that she has been listening in on the whole conversation. 'My husband is unwell at the moment and very tired. Please call back on Tuesday.'

I agree to do so, and hang up.

On the face of it, the man appears to live up to his name. Ill, but not so ill that he's unable to visit his country home a week ago. Ill, but too busy to see me on Monday. Selective amnesia until the pressure is applied. Evasive, in denial, wriggling, seemingly very rattled. I wonder if he'll refuse to see me now that he knows whose son I am. And if he does see me, what is there to stop him simply shooting me another pack of half-truths? After all, he's been a lawyer all his life, a man paid to tailor a suitable version of events for his client.

In the morning I wake from another fitful night with one thought in my mind: I need more information on this man. If I am going to discover the bigger picture, I need another take on this pivotal figure. Though I have no idea if I will find anything, I think it might be worth making one more visit to Tufo.

The old man who, according to Ettore, knows Cesarino is still not home. Nor has the barman's father-in-law returned from Rome yet. It's a gloriously sunny day, so I drive back down the hill to see if I can find the old boy I met near Ettore's house on Friday. Instead of him I meet his niece, a sprightly sixty-year-old. Chatting to her I learn that the one house I have not yet seen – Erico's and Pepina's place – is still standing, though it's difficult to find without a guide. I don't mind. A ramble in the countryside before the old folk return for lunch from their chestnut hunts would be very pleasant. She points me to a dirt track leading down into the valley, across the stream, then off into the countryside.

At first the land is laid to pasture. This gives way to large abandoned vineyards, with dozens of little stone and brick *casetta*s dotted all over the place. Then finally it becomes woodland – thick, shady forest with the occasional wild cyclamen poking up through the leaf mulch. In front I can hear a chain saw at work and the odd shouted remark. Rounding a small bend I come face to face with three pack-mules, heavily laden with cut timber. Their owners are behind them, transferring the wood from the animals to a tractor-drawn trailer on the dirt road. I ask if there is a house up in front and they say that there is. They don't know who used to live there, though. As I pass them I overhear one remark to the other: 'He's English. His father was here in the war.' So, news of the arrival of strangers still passes like lightning round these little rural backwaters.

A few hundred metres further on I come to a gate leading to a cleared meadow. The old house, built of a lovely soft yellow stone, stands at the top of the clearing, above vegetable patches and a small vineyard. I know Dad and Claude slept in the wine cellar here, so I try all the doors on the ground floor, but none budge. A very rickety set of wooden steps at the front of the house leads to three bedrooms on the first floor. Some roof tiles have fallen in, letting the light into the ruined rooms, all decorated in forties style, probably just as they were when Dad was here. As I retie the string holding the upper door shut, a fearful barking erupts below me. I wonder if someone is coming to see who this intruder is, but then I realize that the barking is actually coming from a locked outhouse. The barking continues, rather apathetically, as I make my way back down the track.

Approaching the road, I see the old boy I was hoping to meet, sitting on a bank near his sheep pen. He had heard the dog barking across the valley and, knowing I must be there, decided to wait. He introduces himself as Otello. His first suggestion is a beer at his house. I am warm from the walk and readily accept. This makes him chuckle. 'I know you *Inglesi*, you see. Never refuse a beer – always prefer it to wine, don't you?' This is not strictly true, but I am immediately drawn to this ex-prisoner and keen observer of British drinking habits. We set off, at a staggeringly slow pace, towards his house, a huge building on the left of the road.

As we approach he tells me that his brother and sister-in-law were here throughout the war, and his brother's wife, Domenica, still lives here. He says she certainly remembers Dad well, as he often came to eat with the family. We extract a dusty bottle of beer from a lovely, cool, dark *cantina* (kept specifically for passing Brits, I suspect) and hobble slowly to the first floor. Here is the old lady, who sits me down and immediately places a large pot of fried meat and potatoes in front of me. Despite my protests she insists upon ladling a large portion out onto a plate under my nose. It smells wonderful, so I dutifully eat while the old pair talk. Somewhere, she says, she has a letter from one of the prisoners (not my father), to the

Allies, to be handed in for compensation. Like so many others they didn't want anything for looking after the prisoners, so they kept the letter as a memento. And it was not just prisoners here: in the war there were forty people living in this house, all Italians. This intrigues me, so old Otello explains that at that time the countryside round Rome was seething with misplaced persons, individuals on the run from the Fascists, dodging the call-up to the Fascist militia; whole families fleeing from the starving towns and cities, and from the heavy Allied bombing. Then there were others such as student activists who had taken shelter in the countryside too.

'Students like Cesarino, you mean?' I ask.

'Yes. He was the one who betrayed your father, wasn't he?'

I nod.

'He and his brother got themselves into big trouble with the Germans,' says the old lady, a little sadly. 'The Germans were furious with them for some reason – threatened to shoot them. So they came down here and stayed in this house for a few days to keep out of sight. They used to go up to see your dad and little Claudio in the daytime, but they slept down here. Then their mother went and begged the Germans not to kill her boys, and they seemed to change their minds. The boys went back to the village. That was just a short time before the raid, when Cesarino took the Germans up there to get your father.'

This certainly makes sense, though, try as they will, the old pair can't remember exactly what Cesarino had done to upset the Germans. I ask if the Germans came here during the war.

The old lady looks even more sad. 'Yes,' she says. 'They came many times. They would bash the doors down with their rifles. They pretended they were looking for prisoners, but they really came to steal our food and wine. They took whatever they fancied, *porca miseria!* They did the same thing in Nespolo, just over on the other side of that hill, but there one man got furious. The Germans tried to molest his daughter, so he grabbed a gun and shot three of them. A few days later the Germans came back and they took thirty of the young people of the village, all lovely young men and women. They killed them all. Ten Italians for each German killed. That is what they thought of us, how they treated us.'

I shudder.

Then it is Otello's turn: 'The Germans raided the village again after they took your father, only this time they ordered a curfew. Everyone was to stay put at home while the search party went round. One young lady, my cousin Ana Maria, went out to fetch some water from the village well. They shot her dead on the spot. Her husband rushed out to help his wife, so they shot him dead too, right next to the village well. Ah, what a waste, what a disgrace!'

The shadows hang on their faces for a moment, but then the old lady breaks into a broad smile. 'How wonderful it was to see your father when he came back after the war. The moment he set foot in the valley we all knew, and we came down to Vincenzo's house to see him and your mother. He was still very thin indeed, but your mother was strong, *robusta*. We were all so glad he was alive. I think he said he had escaped again – is that right?'

'He got out once more up north, on the Lombardy

plain, somewhere near Padua, but he was only free for a few days. All that northern area was still controlled by the Fascists, and they hunted him down. Then they shipped him off to Germany. In the end he did manage to cross the lines and meet the Americans, just before the end of the war.' I pause for a moment as they nod, smiling, before I ask: 'And what happened to people like Cesarino after the war? Were they punished, or did they get away with it?'

Otello replies: 'Cesarino was gone by the time I got back from England. I think he left here before the war ended. But he was under the protection of the Germans, so nobody touched him while they were still here. After the war a few collaborators were denounced and the Partisans shot a few Fascists who had been especially evil in the war. But mostly we just went back to our farms. We were all glad it was over and done with. Everyone in the village, all the old people, know what Cesarino did, but he still comes here occasionally. I think he has family nearby. We don't forget, but we have let it become the past.'

It seems an eminently sensible line to take, as long as you or your immediate family have not suffered directly at the hands of a turncoat. My problem is that my father did.

On the other hand, practically everywhere I have stopped on this journey I have been told chilling tales of German atrocities, meted out on Italian civilians and Allied POWs alike. There is no doubt in my mind that the sort of horrors the old couple have just recounted could be replicated thousands of times all over occupied Italy. To keep a hostile, occasionally rebellious population cowed, the Germans repeatedly massacred, tortured, deported, looted. It was quite simply a reign of terror. Their contempt for the Italians, their total lack of scruples and their attested brutality meant that once a couple of suspect eighteen-year-old students fell into their hands the two stood almost no chance of resisting. The wretchedness and guilt that Cesarino must have felt was evidently matched only by his fully justified terror of the Germans. Even Dad and Claude felt that terror, for several overlong minutes up at *Casa Nostra*, while the German major played cat-and-mouse with their lives.

As I drive back to Maria's, I realize that this gentle, careful conversation with the old couple has given me what I need: a context within which to place Cesarino, a much better idea of what he must have been going through.

It is Monday afternoon. Maria's nephew, 'little Angelo', a charming retired *carabiniere*, has invited Maria and me to eat his home-made pizza this evening. I watch, mesmerized, as he smooths out the dough, applies the toppings, and slides them carefully into the open oven, then turns them every few seconds, to get an even bake. He doesn't burn brambles, though, just ordinary wood. It's a relief not to talk about the war much and to savour the best pizza I have ever eaten. I decide to call Cesarino the next morning, go into Rome if he will see me, or head back home to Tuscany if not.

CHAPTER EIGHTEEN

I CALL CESARINO ON TUESDAY MORNING, BUT GET NO reply. I try again later and there's still no answer. On the third attempt a female voice tells me he is not available. I am being cold-shouldered. So I say fond farewells to Maria and heft my pack down to the little village square. There sits the old cripple in his customary spot, just where the Germans lined up the villagers of Vivaro Romano on 17 January 1944. I head for Fiumicino, return the car, then take the train to Tuscany.

Marcello meets me at the station and takes me to our house. I keep calling Cesarino. I have prepared a list of questions for him, but realize, once I have them down, that they contain many words which I simply do not know in Italian. I have never needed to talk about *guilt, lies, betrayal, traitors, regrets, trouble, suspects* or *under arrest*, so I have to acquire a whole new vocabulary for my interview with him. I still feel very ambiguous about meeting him, but without doing so I know that I cannot really bring things to a conclusion. And I do want an end. I heed the wisdom of Lorna Sage's point in *Bad Blood* that a writer of non-fiction should be wary of tying up too many loose ends – endings that are too pat are the work of fiction, not the product of experience. But as surely as night follows day, we all want an ending of some sort, a break in the flow of consciousness, a change of direction, of vision. Once the matter of Cesarino is resolved, I want to walk away from all that war, all those pealing, crumbling memories, and start afresh, stare into the dawn and ask myself what this new day brings.

Dad's travails were not yet at an end, however.

After a night at the major's headquarters, the Germans sent Claude and him to L'Aquila, the squalid transit camp they passed through after they were drugged and recaptured the previous December. Luckily the entire German staff had been changed and no-one recognized them. They decided to masquerade as 'other ranks', as they thought their chances of escape were better than from the officers' quarters. They rapidly befriended a charming cockney SAS sergeant known as 'Smoky' (Sgt Smoker), who had managed to smuggle a spectacular escape knife into the gaol, and plots were hatched immediately. But the strain, at least on Dad, was beginning to tell. About a week later, the night of an aborted escape attempt, he revealed his true feelings in uncharacteristically candid fashion. The plan was simple: cut a hole in the wire at the least visible spot and crawl out at dead of night.

I went to bed in a state of suppressed excitement. Although I had escaped three times already, I was no more inured to it now than I had been last September. I have never considered myself a man of action. I harbour no longing for adventure, and I found these constantly recurring escape crises an intolerable strain on the nerves. This time I did not consider chucking my hand in, because the alternative was even worse. I knew that if Claude and Smoky succeeded, and I was left behind in this foul transit camp, I should never forgive myself. I was, however, far from happy about this unusually desperate scheme. Claude and Smoky, I felt sure, would set about it with the utmost competence. If they managed to snip the wire unobserved, they would slide through as quickly and smoothly as a couple of snakes. But when it came to my turn I was far less confident. I am a naturally awkward person and my wounded hand has rendered me more so. If I succeeded in crawling through two small holes in two barbed wire fences, without getting caught up and giving the show away, it would be nothing short of a miracle.

I was unable to sleep. I tried to think of other things and failed. Again I was afraid, more afraid than before a battle, scared stiff of death or mutilation. The same futile, persistent conjectures, which I have tried to describe before, pursued themselves endlessly through my mind. In five hours from now we may be free again . . . by tomorrow morning I may be dead . . . the world will go on just the same as usual, but I shall not be here . . . blackness . . . unconsciousness . . . annihilation . . . void.

At 2 a.m. a shadow loomed up beside my bunk and a hand touched me on the shoulder. Claude's voice whispered.

'Time to go.'

I got up, put on my trousers and stuffed my boots between shirt and jacket. Then I joined the others, who were making *a reconnaissance from the washhouse window.*

Outside, everything was quiet. The night was clear, but there was no moon. Owing to the lights, it was at first difficult to spot the sentries, but when our eyes became accustomed we saw that at any rate the one in this corner was in his box.

'OK,' said Smoky. 'Let's move.'

We tiptoed out of the dormitory, threading our way through the crowded double-tier bunks, to the staircase. Halfway down the stairs was a window. We paused for a last look.

'My God!' whispered Smoky. 'Look in that corner. There's another blasted sentry.'

He was standing in the shadow of the corner of the compound, only a few yards from the point where we had planned to make our break.

'Well, that's that,' said Claude gloomily.

I must confess that I felt inordinately grateful to that Jerry. My first thought was that I should see the sun again next morning. But when we were once more back in bed, and I was trying to get to sleep, I found myself wishing we had been given that chance. By now it would have been all over. Either we should have been killed, or else we should be tramping happily over the hills, towards an enormous contadini *breakfast. As it was, we should have to wait until 11 a.m. for three meagre slices of black bread which must last us twenty-four hours.*

A few weeks later, Dad, Claude and Smoky did succeed in making a break, but they were soon picked up and this time they were sent to a permanent prison camp in Germany. There, to his bitter regret, Dad was separated from Claude and Smoky, who were both really sergeants, though Claude had been masquerading as a lieutenant for a long time. As 'other ranks' they could enrol for work parties outside the camp, where they judged their chances of escape were better. Dad ended up in a small officers' camp, Oflag IX A/Z, at Rothenburg, on the Fulda river. It was, apparently, one of the best and most secure POW camps in Germany. There he made little effort to escape, but devoted the next nine months to converting his memorized diaries into a narrative account of his adventures in Italy. Writing, once again, became the means of escape, the single way out of the hunger, monotony and tedium of captivity, a sort of paper salvation.

But terror and the escaper mode had not yet finally done with him. As the Western Front collapsed in spring 1945, Oflag IX was evacuated and the prisoners marched east under guard. Passing through a thick forest, Dad and a chum called George made a dash for it and got away unscathed. But they were picked up the next day by a German artillery unit out cutting firs to camouflage their field guns. The escapers were taken to the local town and handed over to the commander of the garrison, a certain Oberleutnant Rex. He placed them in the civilian gaol until the Americans, only a few miles away, began to shell the town. Rex then allowed them and a motley crowd of fellow prisoners, refugees and forced labourers to shelter in a cellar. At that point they were discovered by a *Kampfgruppen* unit, soldiers described by Dad as fanatical Nazis who were bound by a special oath to die rather than surrender.

*

To the Germans, we must have looked a scruffy gang of desperadoes as we emerged, unwashed, unshaven, and in our stockinged feet. To us, these members of the dreaded Kampfgruppe, *armed with pistols, rifles, and light automatics, appeared no less villainous than we had been led to believe. Yells of 'Amerikanische! Amerikanische!' greeted us directly they saw our khaki uniforms. They concluded that we were part of an American patrol which had infiltrated into Bebra during the night. Both George and I kept repeating 'Kriegsgefangene!' [prisoners of war] but they were much too excited to listen. And we knew what happened to spies who were caught in the front line.*

Revolvers were thrust in our backs and we were hustled out into the square. The German in charge gesticulated toward the wall. The soldiers, whom he had detailed as a firing party, were releasing the safety catches on their rifles. So this, then, was the end. We were all, even the Mexican, past caring. Then suddenly came a roar of rage from behind us and we turned, to find Oberleutnant Rex in our midst. But he looked so smart, so Prussian and so angry that we hardly recognized in him the tired and dispirited old man of the previous evening. He gave us a quick glance then turned on the Kampfgruppe. *What, in God's name, were they doing with his prisoners? How dared they interfere in what was none of their business? To be paraded about like a circus by a lot of ignorant, stupid privates? The* Kampfgruppe *had sprung to attention and was clicking its heels and stammering out apologies. They were extremely sorry, Herr Oberleutnant . . . Yes, Herr Oberleutnant, they were certainly at fault. They had not realised that these men were prisoners . . . they thought they must be Americans . . . they—*

*'Enough!' interrupted the Oberleutnant, and marched us
straight back to our cosy, lousy little cell in the jail. How
attractive it looked!*

This all took place on the fourth of April 1945. On the
fifth, the Germans withdrew from Bebra without a fight,
and Dad and George made it to the American lines. By
the sixth, exactly two years after his capture and a year
after Cesarino's betrayal, the Front had moved on, so Dad
found a car, drove back to Bebra and collected his manu-
script from the gaol. On the seventh he and George were
flown to Brussels, and on the morning of the eighth of
April 1945 they landed at Croydon airport. Dad was one
of only a handful of British officers to make a 'home run'
from Germany. That was the last Dad saw of the war outside his head, but it was far from over within.

When he returned to the UK he soon fell into the
depths of despair, a predicament labelled by himself and
his doctors as a severe nervous breakdown. It was complicated by his refusal, or disinclination, to eat, which left
him terribly thin and weak. He weighed about eight
stone. Two years of 'the constant threat of death',
culminating in being put up against a wall to be shot,
would, I think, unnerve most people. The severity of
Dad's condition meant that he had no choice but to
succumb, but there was also a measure of honesty, not
denial, in this collapse. It was an admission, in itself an act
of bravery. At a time when millions of young men had
undergone similar trauma, the prevalent ethos was the
stiff upper lip; the advice to the wobbly young ex-
combatant was: 'Best just to forget it.' Fifty years later we
have a far better understanding of the longer-term

consequences of such repression. A whole generation grew up with massive gaps in their relationships with their fathers. Far too many young men silently dragged their nightmares with them to the ends of their lives. In first succumbing, then rebuilding himself through the catharsis of writing, Dad purged himself of at least some of the horror that had invaded him.

I never talked to him directly about his breakdown, but on one occasion he chose to tell me a little about it. I was sixteen, a fully fledged rebellious adolescent, a child of the sixties, and I rowed endlessly with my mother. She would yell at me; I would answer back. I'd tell her to get stuffed and either roar off from the house on my scooter or storm up to my room, slamming doors as I went. One Sunday morning Dad summoned me to the drawing room.

'I know that at the moment you think everything's Mum's fault, that you can't do anything right in her eyes, but I can promise you that's not really the case. Let me explain. After the war, when I had my breakdown, I couldn't understand why I felt so lousy all the time. Then gradually I became more and more convinced that the army was the root of my misery. I was sure that if I got right out of it, resigned my commission, then I would recover quickly. My CO was very understanding. He offered me the choice of staying in on full pay and receiving treatment through the army, or getting out and receiving psychotherapy privately on the outside. I leapt at the chance to leave, but once I had done so I found it made no difference to my condition at all. So I had to face the fact that it wasn't "all the army's fault" that I was in such a mess, and start to look elsewhere for both the problem and the solution. So you see the very fact that you blame your mother for all your problems shows, in a sense, that she is not the sole cause. Let's not discuss this any more. Just you go away and think about it a bit.'

It did the trick. Relations with Mum improved steadily after that. But this brief conversation raised a series of questions which I have pondered for many years. Was Dad somehow equating parenthood with the institution of the army? After the war did he deliberately reject the pseudo-paternal role of the institution he belonged to? He clearly admitted that at the time he blamed 'the army' for his condition, then discovered that he was wrong. So had the POW camp, the direct instigator of his oppression, somehow been transmuted into the army on his return from the war? Whatever the case, his loathing of the oppression imposed by institutional order was transparent. A committed socialist throughout his army career, he was probably the only regular officer in the Black Watch who openly espoused such political views. And throughout his life he remained at heart a rebel, steadfastly refusing to climb corporate structures to advance himself and his career. So perhaps his leaving the army, though it didn't provide the immediate cure he hoped for, was still an essential step in his reaffirmation of himself as an individual, someone with the right to give and take love as a son, husband and father. Not someone who would depend on the false patronage of the institutions who employed him, he turned instead to the intimacy of family bonds, very much as he had experienced with old Camilla's and Angelo's warm household in Vivaro Romano.

Dad's 'taming the dragons within' was greatly helped by his marriage to my mother, which took place on

8 September 1948, exactly five years after Italian Armistice day. The honeymoon in Italy reunited him with all the best, sweetest and most loving people and experiences the war brought him. And I suppose that in the end the birth of his children, and the recasting of his wartime experiences as thrilling tales for small inquisitive minds, was, ultimately, another aspect of the taming, healing process. My brother Simon was born on 6 July 1949, and I followed on 6 April 1951, eight years to the day after his capture in north Africa.

Thirty-three years later, around 6 April 1984, I was filming in Stratford-upon-Avon when I got a message to call my mother urgently. Dad had contracted cancer of the colon in 1982 and it was successfully removed, but at the beginning of 1984 he started vomiting repeatedly. This time the cancer was attacking his oesophagus. Fatally, he had done nothing about it until it was too late. Or so his surgeon said at first. But a few days later the surgeon paid a visit to the Royal College of Surgeons, where he heard from some of his fellows that a few patients with Dad's symptoms had proved to be operable. It was arranged for him to see Dad at 4.15 that afternoon, when they would discuss if Dad wanted to run the risk of trying to get it out. I was asked in an urgent phone call if I could make it to the meeting. It was already 2.30 when I called Mum, but I got in the rental car I had been issued with and drove hell-for-leather across the Cotswolds, making it to the Radcliffe Infirmary in Oxford just in time.

Over the previous few years, as he got frailer, Dad came to rely on me more than he used to. So when the smooth knife man told us he thought Dad might yet have a chance, Dad turned straight to me for my views.

'You've been a gambler all your life, Dad, and you've always seized the chance when it arises. The way things stand now, seems to me you've only got one chance of recovery. There's no hope if you just leave it. What will happen, doctor, if you are not successful?' I asked.

Turning to my father, the surgeon replied: 'This is deep surgery. We have to go in through your abdomen, then open up the solar plexus from within. Any surgery on this scale has a traumatic effect and it will certainly weaken you, whether we succeed or not.'

Traumatic – that word again. Hadn't the poor man suffered enough trauma for one lifetime already? Wasn't it the earlier traumas that were now resurfacing in the form of this ghastly disease? I said none of this, but couldn't repress the thoughts.

In the end Dad agreed to let the knife man give it a go; and they did the op the next day. But it was no good. Once the surgeon got into his thorax, he could see that the cancer had spread all over his lungs and heart; there was far too much to remove. He inserted a plastic tube inside Dad's oesophagus, to try to keep the passage to his stomach open, and sewed him up.

We visited Dad the next morning, a few hours after he'd come round. He already knew that the op had failed and we expected him to be very wretched. He was that familiar grey-yellow colour, with sweat on his forehead, like after the nightmares way back in the fifties. But he was not at all miserable. He explained with a huge smile that as he thought he was coming round from the anaesthetic he found himself floating out of his body up to the ceiling of the ward. Looking down on the recovery room he was delighted to see it transformed into a gorgeous, glittering ballroom. The nurses were suddenly all dressed in ball gowns, and heavenly waltzes filled the air. He had found himself in white tie and tails, gliding round the dance floor like Fred Astaire. His voice was filled with rapture as he recounted this wonderful near-death experience to us and all the fear had just drained away. We listened, and giggled, and struggled to hold back the tears.

He spent June that year at his favourite pastime, watching Wimbledon on the telly. He had been a very fine tennis player himself, actually competing at Junior Wimbledon as a boy. But he was fading fast. He had lost all his flab and most of his musculature. He was lighter now than he had been when he came back from the war. I noticed that on the phone his voice had become high-pitched, without its familiar resonance. I had to travel abroad for work, so I went down to see him at the beginning of July.

He was shockingly thin and I had to support him when he wanted to go to the loo. He insisted he was not in pain, but was very annoyed that both whisky and wine now tasted unpleasant. No more 'perkers', then, just opiates from that time on. He dozed after I gave him his pills, and my eyes wandered round the room, coming to light on the four handsome young soldiers whose photo still took pride of place on his chest-of-drawers.

His eyes opened. 'You see, I don't really mind going, Howard, as long as it doesn't hurt. I've been so much luckier than they were, you know, to have had a second half to my life. But I can't bear the thought of a lot of pain. Howard, I want you to promise me that if things get like that you'll finish me off quickly. Promise me, Howard.'

'I promise, Dad, of course I promise. No more pain, I promise.' I turned away, hiding the tears.

The GP called round in the afternoon, and when he came down from Dad's room I invited him to sit down for a moment. I told him of my conversation with Dad and asked him if he would be prepared to give me a lethal dose if I requested it. He was a very kind, gentle man and he assured me that it wouldn't be necessary. Nowadays, he said, pain management is so sophisticated that Dad would not suffer, and anyway he would up Dad's medication as the occasion demanded until, he sighed, to be honest, in the end it would be the opiates that laid him to rest. I asked him how long Dad had. The reply was: 'Weeks, not months.' The deep trauma of the chest surgery had weakened him greatly and he could no longer put up much of a fight.

Two weeks later I was in Portland, Oregon, finishing a filming recce, when the call came. Mum said he was slipping fast and I should return immediately. It was Thursday, and I made it back to Oxford by Saturday morning. At the same time my youngest sister, Fiona, arrived from New York. We went to see him together. He had aged twenty years in two weeks and looked ninety years old. Mum told him in a loud voice that Howard and Fiona were here and he swam through the opiates to consciousness.

'Lovely to see you both. You look very healthy and brown.' He smiled. Then, after a few murmured hums and hahs, he slipped back out of consciousness for the last time.

We took it in turns to sit with him. Sunday afternoon was Mum's and my shift. She sat holding his hand. His breathing had become very shallow. Then she murmured:

'His hands have gone very cold – his circulation is failing; it won't be long now.'

I left the room to call my sister Jan, who wanted to be there at the end. But just a few minutes after I returned, he stopped breathing. An exhalation, a pause, then one more inhalation. Another pause, then a short letting out of breath, and it was finished. Death had now got Daddy, once and for all. I sat still, waiting for my mother. She remained holding his hand serenely for several minutes, then told me to go and tell the nurses. It was over.

Many people attended the funeral and the wake at my parents' cottage afterwards. Dad had lots of old and dear friends, and he inspired loyalty in all of them. My two closest friends came too, partly to support me, but mostly because they, too, genuinely liked Dad, had enjoyed his warmth and humour over a glass of wine at the farm in Tuscany, or on the racecourse in Oxfordshire. My mother and we children grieved deeply, felt terrible pain at the loss, but quite suddenly, and very privately, I found myself feeling rather guilty. Why guilty? A totally unexpected sensation had arisen in me. I felt liberated, set free in a very strange way. I realized that up until this point I had never examined a situation, never taken a decision, without subconsciously assessing it as if I were Dad. 'If I was Dad, I'd do this, say that . . .' would flash through my mind, almost involuntarily. Sometimes, of course, when I really wasn't sure what to do I would ring him and get his advice. Now both these options had gone, and I had to think and act for myself. There was no need to seek his approval any more. It was a very strange, disturbing

266

sensation to experience so soon after his parting, but I cannot deny it.

Yet as the weeks and months turned into years and decades after his death, that subconscious mechanism – taking his perspective – didn't go away. I began to see how history and personality are inextricably entwined. It was this entanglement that finally led me to pick up my father's trail as he passed through the agonies and ecstasies of escape and capture in wartime Italy, and to try to identify the legacies his wartime experiences have left me.

CHAPTER NINETEEN

DONE BUT NOT DUSTED. JUST WHEN I THINK I AM finished, the book starts to talk to me. It is 24 January 2002, a bitterly cold evening. An open fire is burning in the grate in our house in London when the phone rings. Ettore Lustrati is calling from Rome. He sounds very excited. He says his sister Nicolina has just given him a copy of a piece she has written in response to a radio programme requesting personal accounts of the war in Italy. I should switch my fax on and he will send it through to me.

I do so, and three pages of text arrive. I call him back.

'OK, Ettore, I take your point. Thanks for sending this. I really hope I can come to see your sister in Rome soon.'

'Do. She told me she would like that. *Ciao*, Osvaldo.'

I turn to the fax. The account is simply titled: *La Mia Guerra*. It tells of her family and farm, which remained free of the war until Christmas 1943, when two frightened POWs turned up on the doorstep of their farm. Her family fixed up a hut for them to live in and she and her sister and little brother took food up to their prisoner friends whenever there was any to spare. Then one day in April 1944 they heard that the Germans were raiding Tufo. She says there were several Jewish families there who had run away from Rome. Some managed to hide, but many were caught. They were betrayed by a spy, she says. The Germans then began to search the countryside.

The Germans, as we feared, did not take long to arrive; accompanying them was another evacuee from Rome, who had informed the Germans of everything which was happening in our area. This included some huts which the young people of the village had built deep inside the woods and which were totally inaccessible to outsiders. The Germans used dogs first, who sank their teeth into those they found inside; then they set fire to the huts and destroyed everything.

I see it again, as if it were now, with infinite sadness, against the outline of the hill, lit up by the evening sun: Ian, with his hands raised, leaving the little house which for a short time had been his refuge. Following him was his friend Claude, and immediately behind him came the Germans, brandishing their machine guns.

She writes that the Germans never came back in force; just a few stragglers hid there for a few days as the German army retreated. On the first of June they learned that the Germans had withdrawn and the war was over. So if Cesarino hadn't betrayed them, Dad and Claude would have hooked up with the Allies within weeks.

By the time Dad returned to visit the valley, Nicolina had married and was living in the north of Italy, so she never saw him again. But she was delighted that he came back to visit his Italian friends, adding: *Nothing and nobody could ever make us forget all the things that we saw in those days*.

I resolve that before too long I will take myself off to Rome to finish this business, to try again to confront Cesarino and to meet Nicolina: the darkness and the light.

A bumper olive harvest summons me back to Italy in November 2002, a little over two years after I started this project. Now I want it done with, loose ends tied up and my face firmly turned in a new direction.

The farm is cold and damp but the work is enjoyable, and it's always a treat to spend entire days outside in the fresh air with Marcello. In the evening I drive up to the village to use the phone. First I call Elena Nulli at the farm in Botto. She is delighted that I am coming to see them all and readily agrees to get her son-in-law to make a photocopy of the Italian translation of Dad's book for me. Adriana is pleased that I am coming, but feigns irritation that I am not bringing my wife and all our children to stay for several days. Maria Cerini, in Vivaro Romano, is a little confused about who is calling, until I remind her that I am *'figlio del Capitano Gianni'*, then it all comes back to her and she insists I must come to stay. Ettore Lustrati is delighted that I am coming to Rome to see him and Nicolina, and agrees to fix up a large family lunch at his apartment in Rome.

Cesarino sounds more healthy and alert than last year, but even more suspicious. 'Are you really the person who called me a few months ago? Please give me some identification,' he demands in a weaselly voice.

'Certainly. I am the son of the English officer who knew you in the war. On the sixth of April 1944 you led the Germans to a *casetta* near Tufo where he was—'

'Yes, OK, very well,' he interrupts. 'Now I know who you are.'

I ask to meet him. Again.

'Not possible this week, too busy. Call me back on Thursday next week. I might be able to see you on Friday.'

Friday is the day I fly back to England, but not until the evening. Somehow, though, I am convinced that the possibility will not materialize. He doesn't want to say 'no', but I doubt there will ever be a 'yes'. 'No', after all, would be tantamount to admitting guilt, not an exercise lawyers enjoy, I suspect.

I pick olives for a few more days, until we have enough to make plenty of oil for all the family, then I head south for Orvieto. Soon Chiusi is on my left, then Città della Pieve, where Dad and Tom were recaptured. Next I am on the raised section of motorway where we all so narrowly escaped death's clutches in 1964. Minutes later the turning to Orvieto looms. Like driving through a landscape of ghosts.

I skirt round the southern edge of the city and find the Botto turning without difficulty. Arriving at the Nulli farmhouse, all is unusually quiet; only Elena is at home. She wraps me in her enormous smile and takes me by both shoulders after our greeting kisses.

'You're a bit fatter,' she says approvingly, then leads me into the farmhouse, where once again I must sit in my father's place at the table, drink his favourite wine and chat about the children and grandchildren as if I (or do I mean 'he'?) had never been away.

All is well. One of the girls has just had her first baby, a little girl. They are both thriving and, thank the Lord, the baby sleeps. Young Giacomo, by now four years old, is still *molto bravo*.

'Every day when he comes back from the nursery he tells me long stories about the other children and the teachers and the things he has been doing. He loves to sit on my lap and tell his granny all the things he has observed that day. I think he's very bright, little Giacomo.' I have no doubt she is right.

I drive over to Canale to say hello to Adriana Nulli and her husband, and give them copies of some photos Mum took in Botto on their honeymoon in 1947, and a copy of the photo of Dad and his three chums in full dress uniform, taken in 1936. Like everyone else, she recognizes him immediately, because he is so much taller than the other three. An intense stare at his face produces a quick smile, that sudden flash of recognition as she marries up this face with the one of her memories, when she was just six years old. A single tear forms in the corner of her eye and is quickly dabbed away by her handkerchief.

By the time I get back to the farmhouse the new-born baby and her proud mother and father have arrived, as has Giacomo the brave, his father Alberto, two more of Elena's daughters and a bevy of her grandchildren. As usual, a cheerful din prevails.

Alberto seats me at the head of the table and fetches a bottle of his *abboccato* sparkling white wine. We talk of the *vendemmia*, the grape harvest (poor vintage throughout Italy this year, too much rain in September), and of the olive harvest (excellent in most places, as long as you sprayed against the olive 'fly' in August). Elena gets out her glasses and the children cluster round as we inspect the photos and try to figure out who the people are. Ilario and his parents we are sure of, but nobody quite knows who the other people are in a group photo with Dad at Botto.

The photocopy of the translation of Dad's book duly arrives and I glance briefly at it. It opens with a brief 'declaration' by the translator, who has signed it, though it's not easy to read the signature. It looks like *'Claudio* [or *Claudia*] *Todiani, Orvieto, Agosto 1955'*. Thereafter it seems to be a verbatim translation of Dad's text. I glance at the 'declaration', but there is too much hubbub all around me, so I decide to leave it until later. I ask Elena if I may use the phone, but when I call Cesarino I get the answerphone. So after fond farewells and promises to bring the family to visit, I head on south, towards Maria and Vivaro Romano.

On the motorway, where concentration is one hundred per cent but automatic, my mind wanders to Cesarino. I've seen his name in inverted commas in the translator's 'declaration' but haven't had time to discover the context. I still feel very ambiguous about him. Part of me wants to meet him, to hear his 'confession', to understand who or what forced him to betray Dad. Another, more cynical side of me suspects that if he will talk at all it will be to say that he was forced to do it. But how can I be sure without asking him and looking into his eyes that he didn't voluntarily betray Dad, as well as the hiding places of some of the young people of Tufo? Part of me wants to take Maria's advice, draw a line under it, forgive and forget. Another part of me says: 'Don't let him get away with it. Force the truth out of him.'

I leave the motorway at Carsoli and find a very patient lady with a hand-loadable photocopier. It takes her nearly half an hour to make Maria's copy of the book. It's dusk as I leave the little town on the plain. I can see twinkling in front and above me the lights of Vallinfreda and Vivaro Romano as they cling to their hillsides like eagles' eyries.

Maria peers down from her flower-filled balcony and beams as I call out her name. The hallway leading to the stairs to her flat stinks of tomcats just as it did last year, but upstairs all is clean and pleasant. Within minutes of my arrival a huge plate of ham, salami, olives and artichokes is thrust before me, along with a good bottle of red wine she has bought from the village grocer for me. I protest feebly that it is only five o'clock, but am dismissed with a sweep of the arm as Maria sits down next to me. She gets stuck in, eating heartily, evidently enjoying the treats as much as her guest.

Thin slices of veal fried in olive oil and a little Marsala follow, with a green salad. As Maria eats, she stares at the photo of Dad I brought for her, muttering: 'He was such a gentleman, your father, such a perfect gentleman.' Taking the copy of the typescript I have brought, she glances briefly at it, then puts it to one side, evidently to be savoured later. I show her briefly where she can find the chapters on Dad's time here with her, but it's quite obvious that she means to read from cover to cover, after I've gone, and take her time over it. She tells me how wonderful it is to have at last an Italian translation of the book, since her English edition has sat dumbly on her shelf, unread, for the last half-century. It makes me feel good too: a loose end tied up; a small repayment for her enormous kindness to Dad in the war.

I beg the use of the phone. Ettore is all set up for tomorrow, and arranges a rendezvous point at a turning off the *Anulare*, Rome's ring road, for the next morning. Cesarino's number is once again manned by the answerphone. I try again two hours later, with the same result. A very busy 79-year-old, this, apparently nearly always out of the house, after my first, unexpected call.

At nine I make my excuses and move down to my apartment. Maria has already switched on the heating and made my bed. Small kindnesses . . . as always.

I settle down on the sofa to take a look at the translator's note and quickly find my pulse racing. The translator has decided to 'hint at' the reasons why the book has not been published in Italian.

The reasons lie in a decision taken from above to protect the reputation of the reactionary classes, and especially that of . . . somebody very close to the then Prime Minister.

Already the English-language edition had been made to disappear from circulation in Italy by a purchase in bulk, which is a cheering example of the way our government leaders use the money they've been entrusted with by the Italian people.

My God. Somebody deliberately blocked the circulation of the book by buying up every copy of it. So why didn't the distributors just order a further shipment of the book? I think I know the answer to this: the book was published in English in 1947. It got tremendous reviews and the short print run sold out in just a few weeks. But in this post-war period there was an acute shortage of paper, so it wasn't reprinted. By the time the Italian distributors had got back to Gollancz, there would have been no copies left.

I knew nothing of any of this. Dad never told me that there had been an Italian version of the book, nor anything about the suppression of the English edition back in 1947. When I got back to England last year I told Mum that Cesarino was alive and she remembered that Dad had got very angry when he heard that Cesarino was standing for public office. He tried to stop it happening, but evidently didn't succeed. After the war Italy was not an occupied country. Unlike the Germans and the Japanese, the Italians were largely left to reconstitute their own government. And the 'reactionary classes' were still a strong force to be reckoned with. Regrouping under the banner of the Christian Democrats, they could not sensibly re-elect their old fascist leaders, so there was plenty of room for ambitious, smart younger members of the political right to advance their careers rapidly. It's a matter of public record that the young lawyer Dr Cesare Dall'Oglio was one of the people who took advantage of this situation, despite Dad's efforts to thwart him.

I go to bed with my head reeling. At least tomorrow I will be getting together with people who knew both Dad and Cesarino, and who were there to witness the wartime activities of both of them.

'When you get to the ring road, turn left towards Fiumicino airport. The first service station you'll see is an

AGIP. Just after it is the turn-off to Via Casilina. Take that. I'll be waiting for you on the slip road at ten o'clock.'

Ettore is there. I follow him through a maze of little suburban streets until he pulls up outside a small block of flats. He owns two of them, rents one out and lives in the other. His wife greets me warmly and asks if I like wild mushrooms. I remind her that I've already been mushrooming with Ettore and, yes, I love them. Mushroom pasta to start with, then, followed by lamb, roasted in chunks, with rosemary and garlic. Nothing beats it.

Ettore and I go down to his *cantina*, a little underground cellar, and fish out three bottles of his best sparkling wine, then he drives me down to the local photocopying shop. We make copies of the translation for him and for his older sister, Nicolina. As we return she and her daughter are just drawing up in a smart new Audi.

A strong, robust woman, with big smile and handshake, she looks much younger than her seventy-five years. I feel I already know her a little through her story of befriending and caring for Dad and Claude, and her moving eyewitness account of Cesarino's betrayal and their capture by the Germans.

By now I am used to the cordial protocol: the family chat, the listing of the children and grandchildren. She knows of Dad's farm in Tuscany and she'd heard from her brother Ettore about my mother and my own family, so there was much to work our way through. Ettore pops a cork and pours his best *frizzante*, and slowly we come round to her account of the family first seeing and sheltering Dad and Claude, of all the fun they had together.

'Your father used to cross two sticks and do a hilarious dance over the top of them,' Ettore interjects. 'He would leap and scream and we'd all fall about laughing.'

Just as I had done as a child. Dad had learned sword dancing while stationed in the Highlands in the Black Watch, and he was a natural at this exuberant art form. We chuckle together in the suburban Roman apartment, bound by a shared memory. I see my father, hands held high above his head, feet leaping and toes pointing, a Highland reel on the gramophone, his claymore and its scabbard crossed on the floor, and hear the ear-piercing shrieks he let loose as he bounded and whirled round and over the crossed swords. It all comes rushing back to me, for just a moment.

Nicolina reaches the point in her story where she sees Dad and Claude being marched away by the Germans, and her and my eyes mist over. But then she breathes deeply and continues: 'I suppose it might have been a blessing for us. Because if they hadn't taken your Dad and Claude, they would have come looking for them at our place. I was fifteen then and my older sister was twenty-two. Heaven knows what they would have done to us if they'd come to our house.'

We pause, and sigh, and agree.

'We could see the smoke rising from the hut, and that really worried us. Poor old Mr Delfa kept all his hay, all his winter fodder for his animals, in the next-door room. He would have been ruined if it had caught fire. So as soon as we were sure the Germans had gone we raced up to the *casetta*. They had set fire to the double mattress old Pepina had given your dad, so we rushed to the spring to fetch water and managed to put the fire out before it spread to the hay.'

'And you know what?' adds Ettore. 'When your dad came back after the war, you know what he had with him? He had a brand-new double mattress, which he gave to old Pepina to make up for the one the *Tedeschi* burned.'

Another small kindness repaid. Well done, Dad.

Nicolina turns to me and explains that now we have all met up she would like me to have a complete copy of her account, 'My War', including some paragraphs Ettore had 'edited' from the end. I read them quickly.

She knows of Dad's book and gives its correct title in Italian – *Prigioniero alla Macchia*. I ask her how she knows the title and she replies that Dad sent the title to her family in the early 1950s. But, she states, the book was withdrawn immediately after its publication. She goes on to state that her family 'got to know' that 'someone' had intervened again and blocked the publication of the book, explaining that this was not the sort of story that the political establishment wanted to read. She doesn't give a name to the offender. Her statement is typed, and signed by her.

As we talk, I feel my attitude to Cesarino change, harden. That ambiguity, that desire to find a justification for his behaviour, is no longer relevant. Here was a man who seems to me to have played life's cards for his own advancement. I believe that I now have the measure of the man.

The lamb exceeds even my highest expectations and draws the conversation away from war, treachery and such indigestible matters. Ettore tells me he has an allotment just outside the city, where he makes his wine and olive oil and grows all his own vegetables. Would I like to see it? Of course I would. We drive out there in the late afternoon and I get time to go over the day's developments in my head.

I no longer wish to see him. I am convinced that if we meet he will try to conceal the truth from me. Though it's only hearsay that he was involved in the block purchase of the English edition of the book in Italy, and the suppression of the Italian version, let the facts speak for themselves:

1. There is no question whatsoever that Cesarino Dall'Oglio betrayed my father to the Germans on 6 April 1944. His motives for doing so remain obscure, though personal gain or advancement cannot be ruled out.

2. The English-language edition of Dad's book was apparently subject to a bulk aequisition by person(s) unknown shortly after its arrival in Italy in 1947, effectively blocking its circulation there.

3. The book was translated in its entirety into Italian, at least by 1955, but it was never published there, for reasons unknown.

This raises a simple question: who stood to gain by facts 2 and 3?

The German who murdered Tom was never identified, in the book or elsewhere, and I hardly think Lieutenant Schreiter would have travelled to Italy in 1947 and again in 1955 to protect his good name as a security officer in a lousy transit POW camp.

But for me a much more important question is: who has lost as a result of facts 2 and 3? Dad wrote his book with a very clear objective – to praise and to thank those incredibly kind, brave people who constantly sheltered and protected him and his pals in extremely tough times.

This is the dedication, the first words in the book after its title:

This book is dedicated to the memory of Tom Cokayne, and also, because I know he would wish it, to the peasant people in Italy, who helped us with such unfailing generosity and courage.

These are the people who have lost out as a result of the suppression of Dad's book: the lorry drivers who saw the escapers clear the Apennines; the kind *caribinieri capo* in Florence; the old cobbler who fixed their boots in Lucolena; the incredibly brave woman in Orvieto who rescued Dad after Tom's murder; Ilario and the people of Botto, and Pompilio and Sestilio Nulli, along with their large and boisterous families; the charming tailor Benedetto of Calvi in Umbria, who later paid with his life for aiding the likes of my father; Angelo and Camilla Cerini and their children (Maria Cerini told me of her frustration at having a book that featured her family but she could not read for more than fifty years. Whose fault was that?); the Lustrati family and their neighbours, who took such good care of Dad and Claude for such a long time, and who still remember him with warmth and affection.

These are the people whose brave deeds have gone unheard, unacknowledged, these last fifty years, as a result of someone's decision to keep the whole story beyond the Italian public's reach.

My father taught me that the cynical manipulation of truth for political ends is the path of fascism, not democracy. That was what he and the Allied powers were

fighting for. That his own work should end up manipu-
lated in this way is a cruel irony. But let's hope now that
the voices of those unsung heroes will be acknowledged at
last, and that the man who betrayed my father to the
enemy will be exposed, albeit very belatedly, for what he
really is. And should anyone out there be thinking of
block-buying this book, please be my guest. This time
there's no paper shortage, and we'd be delighted to keep
resupplying and resupplying our Italian distributors for as
long as you choose to keep taking the books off the
shelves . . .

As night falls, I take my leave of Nicolina Lustrati, the
woman who saw Dad captured in 1944. Her younger
brother leads me out to the motorway. We have promised
to stay in touch – he wants to teach me how to prune my
olive trees next spring. I have promised to bring them
copies of this book – in Italian, I hope – as soon as it's
published. I circle the ring road, almost to Fiumicino
airport, then swing right, heading north up the coast. I
don't feel relieved, I feel deflated, dashed by that sense of
anticlimax I always get when I know something's over. I
don't know why I did it, just that it's done now.

Back at the farm the night is black, the house cold and
damp. I drag Dad's favourite rocking chair through the
kitchen, throw a few sticks together in the hearth and set
light to them. I pour a generous 'perker' (his word) to
warm myself up. Here I am in his house, sitting in his
chair, drinking his favourite dram, and yet almost for the
first time I feel alone. And I'm happy about it.

Going out there, finding the people, seeing the places and
hearing fresh perspectives on the events he had been

through brought me closer to Dad than I had ever imagined possible. And I now feel calm about his experiences – the edgy, gnawing undercurrent they had always stirred in me has disappeared. The bitter fruits are digested, no longer able to stick in my throat. In this sense it may be that I have changed, done some growing, catching up with him.

Many people – professionals such a literary agents, publishers and editors, as well as friends and family – ask me if my view of Dad has changed since I made these memorial journeys. Well, yes. I think I understand much more clearly what he went through, but, no, I don't think my basic view of him has changed. Somewhere in his book, Dad recalls a conversation with a girlfriend before the war. He asks her if he's different when he's had a few drinks. She replies: no, you're still you when you're tight, only more so. And that just about sums it up for me too. He's still Dad, my dad, only more so.